W9-BTA-728

Formation for Ministry

in

American Methodism

Twenty-first Century Challenges and Two Centuries of Problem-Solving

RUSSELL E. RICHEY

Candler School of Theology

Emory University[1]

[1]This study originated as a plenary address at THE UMC AFTER TAMPA: WHERE DO WE GO FROM HERE? *A United Methodist Faculty Consultation for the 2012–16 Quadrennium*, an event sponsored and hosted by Candler School of Theology, Emory University. Cosponsors included the General Board of Higher Education and Ministry, in cooperation with the General Board of Global Ministries, the General Board of Discipleship, the Foundation for Evangelism, and the General Commission on Archives and History. The revision and expansion of the address into book form was aided by a Bianchi Excellence Award from the Emory University Emeritus College, and its support is gratefully acknowledged. Also appreciated are the attention to and affirmation of this revised study by the staff of the General Board of Higher Education and Ministry and, on its behalf, the careful critique by editor Crys Zinkiewicz. Cover design and layout by Nancy Terzian.

Copyright ©2014 by the General Board of Higher Education and Ministry, The United Methodist Church. All rights reserved.

ISBN 978-0-938162-09-4

Produced by the Office of Communications. Manufactured in the United States of America.

Contents

Theological Education
Today's Challenges in Bicentennial Perspective

From John Wesley's commissioning of what named itself the Methodist Episcopal Church to this day, American Methodism has contended with—but prospered through—two powerful, seemingly conflicting social imperatives: **connectionalism** and **localism**! The new church recast Wesley's connectional mission statement in terms apt for the new nation and the yawning American continent.[2] "God's Design, in raising up the Preachers called Methodists," the first *Discipline* indicated, was "To reform the Continent, and spread scripture Holiness over these Lands."[3] Under such a grand, indeed grandiose, connectional vision, American Methodism prospered because it resolutely kept Wesley's class and quarterly conference local ministries and its array of on-the-ground officers and governance structures.

Perhaps no one more demonstratively acclaimed Methodism's connectional-localism than Bishop Francis Asbury, who traversed its length and breadth preaching and praying alongside local leaders. Endeavoring always to hold together the tension of the two imperatives, he contended with powerful localizing and regionalizing divisive tendencies quite prevalent from colonial days on.

Today's United Methodism lives as well with societal currents of connectionalism and localism. They sometimes work famously in tandem and at other times and contexts opt for visions and ministries wedded only to their respective ideal. At interplay in various programs and policies, the two often come dramatically into display at General Conferences. There social and ministerial issues drive parties into intercontinental alliances against changing the denomination's transcontinental policy on homosexuality even though at other points those groups argue against overarching ministry structures and programs for global and national welfare. And vice versa. For example, arguers for local or regional latitude on ceremonies for and ordination of homosexuals sometimes press for internationalizing the denomination's intervention ministries.

One version of the imperatives, important for the future of theological education, might be termed **Post-institutional** (a version of localism); the other (a version of connectionalism), **Digital**. Before noting a few of the potential effects on these two tendencies, I offer a quick reminder that seminaries and preparation for ministry thrive between the two.

Seminary localism? With the exception of the Methodist Theological School in Ohio, which was founded relatively recently (1960), Methodism deliberately "located" its theological schools in urban settings. Most it placed within universities. Its faculties it expects to be significantly engaged in local churches. Seminarians, of course, must have field education. Many serve local churches throughout their programs. In either case, clergy and local church leaders play an incredibly important role in shaping the next generation of ministers. Continuing education as well serves local and regional interests. Befitting their interest and largesse, local laity's names adorn a school's buildings, faculty chairs, scholarship programs, and ministry initiatives. Methodism located its seminaries with an eye on the specific setting and its role in the shaping of the denomination's itinerants.

The consequence of Methodism locating seminaries in university settings or capping its universities with seminaries is that the church's schools now are webbed into an academic, societal, and denominational organizational fabric—fabric connectional, national, or global in texture and purposes. So the schools are dependent on the Ministerial Educational Fund (MEF) and therefore the church's fund-raising apparatus. They are overseen by the General Board of Higher Education and Ministry (GBHEM). Various purposes, services, and mutual programming link them closely with conference and jurisdictional boards of ministry. Singular among American denominations, United Methodism has credentialed and guided educational institutions, among them seminaries, through the doings of the University Senate. Federal largesse and programs, including Work-Study and the various loan programs, make enrollment possible for many students. For their own funding, the schools rely on foundations and in some cases corporations. For field education and credentialing of chaplains-to-be, they relate to hospitals locally and nationally and to other care-giving institutions (through Clinical Pastoral Education and comparable programs). And given their university setting or proximity, the seminaries remain sensitive to the well-being of American higher education generally and increasingly to international theological educational opportunities. UMC seminaries live, breathe, and work in institutional America and a connectional church.[4]

Challenges and Implications

So, **first** what is theological education to make not so much of recent General Conference proposals but of the more enduring anti-bureaucratic, anti-centralized, anti-institutional mood so prevalent in parts of or on specific issues of the church? What of—

- Visions of radical streamlining of the denomination and its agencies?
- Efforts to dismantle the church's corporate structure?
- Proposals to flatten the church and/or disperse its connectional functions?
- Designs for removal or tearing up of denominational infrastructure or fabric?

What follows for theological education and United Methodism from scenarios that endeavour to turn congregations into franchises? What from the privileging of business measures, metaphors, and discourse in church life? What when clergy remake themselves into franchise leasers or managers? their ministry into measurable outputs? the religious life into commodities? our laity into consumers whose "buying" or "not" sets policy?

And, presuming that the anti-institutional mood will birth yet other schemes, that the ecclesial "tea party" spirit will sustain itself, and that other proposals to dismantle United Methodist apparatus will surface—what implications follow for theological education?

- What is the future for seminaries as institutions in an institution-adverse church?
- What follows for apportionments for MEF, for GBHEM, and for connectional oversight of American theological education?
- Are the schools increasingly to be related, not connectionally, but to local ministries, to area Boards of Ordained Ministry (BOM), and to conference-level support systems?
- Does the whole connection simply collapse?
- Is the local church all that is to be left standing?
- And what does this all mean for our notion that we train and ordain into one ministry, one connection, one church?

Methodism established its seminaries, as we shall see, as part and parcel of the late nineteenth century centrally and nationally controlled corporate reconfigurations of church, business, and government. The modern board-and-agency denomination, Methodist universities and hospitals, seminaries, and systematic finance derived from the same reforming spirit. And the theological schools prospered in an institution-creating, institution-friendly church, its crowning achievement being the MEF. What next for seminaries when institutions are deemed liabilities and not assets?

Further and second, what do we make of the incredible opportunities or challenges or threats posed by digital, virtual, online, offsite, mediated instruction?

- of massive open online courses (MOOC) and of the various digital pedagogies and technologies already developed and still emerging?
- of theological education mounted by some of our schools on such platforms?

- of formal and theological educational ventures offered not by Association of Theological Schools (ATS)-accredited seminaries but by mega-churches, conferences, centers, or colleges?
- of teaching and learning no longer governed by or reliant on what has been Methodism's stock in trade—print?
- of libraries no longer featuring physical books?[5]
- of the digitization of a virtual inventory of Methodist literature and serials by the American Methodism Project?
- of the end of Cokesbury-as-store?

Is there a theological Coursera, edX, Udacity, or Udemy looming?[6]
Will GBHEM move its UMC Cyber Campus from "lifelong learning" into developing its own faculty, mounting a full-fledged program for ministry, and replacing all of our seminaries? Its mission:

> The vision for UMC Cyber Campus is to provide *free* theological training resources in multiple languages and to make these resources available globally at a low cost through Internet technology.

> The mission of UMC Cyber Campus is to assist The United Methodist Church in making disciples of Jesus Christ by using online educational tools. The goal is to use these resources to effectively develop leadership for United Methodist clergy and laity.[7]

What now for seminaries in a cyber-educational world?

Toward Solutions—A Bicentennial Perspective

"We've come a long way, baby" and yet in some ways, we may be right back at the beginning or at least further back historically in what now need to be our strategies for doing formation for ministry. We've seen some of these educational platforms before, albeit not in a digital and post-institutional form.

So perhaps let's not despair of our future in ministerial formation but see what we can learn from where we have been.

A word about how I do history and how I'll proceed: Those who have happened on my essays, may have discovered that I have a habit of looking at the long saga of Methodism in terms of stages or phases. The approach, if done crudely—

- obscures the gradual nature of change,
- isolates a few tendencies from a larger constellation,
- ignores countervailing trends,
- selects confirming evidence, and
- overestimates the consensus around selected patterns.

The reader may judge whether the following falls prey to any of these "beasts." I believe the schema offered here to be helpful and not distorting of the history of American Methodist ministerial formation. And it serves heuristic purposes, moving the discussion toward potential solutions. (I should add that it provides an opportunity to revisit and substantially revise a prior typology of Methodist ministerial formation.)[8]

So then an eight-fold historical schema:

Counseled	under Wesley's Imperatives and through books
Collegial	by yokefellowed tutelage
Conferenced	in course-of-study guidance and accountability
Collegiate	for Randolph-Macon, Wesleyan, Emory... formation
Seminary	in training at Boston University, Garrett, Drew...
Synthesized	through courses plus CPE and Field Ed
Contextualized	in pedagogies and curricula shaped by various contexts
Counseled again?	in Wesleyan imperatives—online?

These represent successive stages of ministerial formation. For convenience and simplicity I will focus on developments in the Methodist Episcopal Church (MEC), The Methodist Church (MC), and The United Methodist Church (UMC) and also on formation on full conference member and/or elder. (Formation of the broader stable of ministerial offices from Wesley on would require more time and space than I am allotted here.)

Several further points concerning the classification into stages are important to keep in mind:

1. The first did not disappear when the second emerged; the first and second remained when the third emerged, and so on. The prior ones lingered—the older typically being incorporated, sustained, transfigured, or adapted by the later stages. Consequently, today's patterns, to some extent, build upon and retain aspects of earlier stages.

2. Nevertheless, one can speak of a dominant or policy-setting style in each of the successive periods. So, it is important that we identify the distinctive mark(s), pedagogies, and educational apparatus of the several stages.

3. And, we may want to ask, whether there was theology, an ecclesiology, a vision of the kingdom—perhaps latent—in one or more or each stage? If so, what was gained and what lost when one pattern gave way to another? And might we wish to think theologically about how we construct ministerial formation going forward—perhaps aided by the schema and the several stages.

[Note that the Appendix contains documents related and organized in relation to the eight stages of Methodist ministerial formation, typically quotations too long to be worked readily or completely into the text. The parenthesis (see Appendix) guides the reader to this illustrative material.]

---

[2] Note that this study does limit itself to North American United Methodism and its predecessor denominations and to the training ventures that produced traveling preachers, conference members, and the ordained. The rationale for the focus on formation for ministry rather than the more limited theological education will be more obvious after this introductory section. And in the effort to exhibit the changes in formation for ministry, I reproduce excerpts from critical statements at some length.

[3] Russell E. Richey, Kenneth E. Rowe and Jean Miller Schmidt, *The Methodist Experience in America: A Sourcebook* (Nashville: Abingdon Press, 2000), 1785a, Q. 4. The *Sourcebook* is noted hereinafter as MEA 2 and *The Methodist Experience in America: A History* (Nashville: Abingdon Press, 2010) as MEA 1.

[4] Russell E. Richey, William B. Lawrence and Dennis M. Campbell, eds. and co-authors, *Questions for the Twenty-first Century Church*, (Nashville: Abingdon Press, 1999), vol. 4 of *United Methodism and American Culture*, 5 vols. (Nashville: Abingdon Press, 1997–2005).

[5] *The Wall Street Journal* (February 6, 2013), "Library That Holds No Books."

[6] *The Wall Street Journal* (January 2, 2013) B8, (Feb. 15, 2013) A3, and (Sept. 27, 2013) A3 for three of many articles on MOOC initiatives and issues, the former "Online Courses Look for a Business Model," the second "Web Classes Grapple with Stopping Cheats," addressing an age-old problem hyped to a new level, that of containing cheating in such 'open' ventures and the third "Job Market Embraces Massive Online Courses." See also "Revolution Hits the Universities," *The New York Times, Sunday Review* (January 27, 2013), 1, 11. The *Duke Magazine* carried an article, titled as "Beyond the Classroom: Exploring the Opportunities (and limits) of MOOCs" and also as "MOOC U?" in issue of Summer 2014, 24–31.

[7] See the UMC's online courses at http://www.gbhem.org/site/c.lsKSL3POLvF/b.8510481/k.96EE/UMC_Cyber_Campus.htm.

[8] For an earlier effort to develop such a schema, a simpler one, see Russell E. Richey, *Doctrine in Experience: A Methodist Theology of Church and Ministry* (Nashville: Abingdon Press/Kingswood Books, 2009), 139–56.

Counseled
Under Wesley's Imperatives and Through Books

The earliest colonial preachers—at least those on the Methodist rather than United Brethren (UB) or Evangelical Association (EA) sides—gained what little or much of formation they experienced for ministry on British terms. That would include those who came on their own: Philip Embury, Robert Strawbridge, Captain Thomas Webb, Robert Williams, John King, Joseph Yearbry, and William Glendenning; and those whom Wesley appointed and sent: Richard Boardman and Joseph Pilmore (1769), Francis Asbury and Richard Wright (1771), Thomas Rankin and George Shadford (1773), and James Dempster and Martin Rodda (1774).

When this little band of brothers gathered to plan for ministry in North America, they could not have had very high aspirations about theological or ministerial education. Nevertheless, when they initially convened, they addressed the matter, or at least laid the preconditions for formation of their to-be-recruited American colleagues when they convened. The initial American conference dealt with ministerial formation in two ways.

First, it embraced the authority of Wesley and of the "Large Minutes of the Conference" (the predecessor to *The Book of Discipline*). The following queries were proposed to every preacher:

1. Ought not the authority of Mr. Wesley and that conference, to extend to the preachers and people in America, as well as in Great-Britain and Ireland?
   Answer. Yes.
2. Ought not the doctrine and discipline of the Methodists, as contained in the minutes, to be the sole rule of our conduct who labour in connection with Mr. Wesley in America?
   Answer. Yes.
3. If so, does it not follow that if any preachers deviate from the minutes, we can have no fellowship with them till they change their conduct?
   Answer. Yes.

And secondly, it recognized that the guidance for ministry given by Wesley in Minutes, Hymnbook, and his various other publications required both the accessibility of Wesley's *Works* and their availability under Wesley's or the conference's aegis. To care for that Wesley-controlled access, two of the conference's six ministry-enabling rules, agreed to by all the preachers present, reined in one of their colleagues:

None of the preachers in America to reprint any of Mr. Wesley's books, without his authority (when it can be got) and the consent of their brethren.
Robert Williams to sell the books he has already printed, but to print no more, unless under the above restriction.[9]

From this beginning would follow formation processes that featured at least:

1. Living into Wesley's counsel as set forth in the "Large Minutes" and in its later form as the *Discipline*—counsel mediated in and by books
2. Learning ministry by doing it
3. Being birthed into ministry and nurtured by the community on a circuit, by the saints on successive circuits, by Methodism as a connectional system

4. Growing spiritually in one's gifts, grace, and fruit

These four constituted the foundation for Methodist ministerial formation, then and thereafter, so a few words about each of these facets would seem in order.

Living Into Wesley's Counsel—Books! Books!

Absent the Robert Williams initiative to sell books, getting books for the preachers proved a challenge. In 1781 the conference recognized the problem in responding affirmatively to the query: "Ought not the preachers often to read the Rules of the Societies, the Character of a Methodist, and the Plain Account of Christian Perfection, *if they have got them?*"[10]

Subsequently, in 1783, Francis Asbury appointed John Dickins to New York, where, in undertaking the role of book steward, Dickins put American Methodism in the publishing business, offering an array of books helpful to new ministers and to members (see **Appendix**).[11]

Formalizing that ministerial formation role, the 1787 *Discipline*, "Arranged under proper Heads and Methodized in a more acceptable and easy Manner," concluded with a section "On the Printing of Books, and the Application of the Profits arising therefrom." It specified:

> As has been frequently recommended by the Preachers and People, that such Books as are wanted, be printed in this Country, we therefore propose,
>
> 1. That the Advice of the Conference shall be desired concerning any valuable Impression, and their Consent be obtained before any Steps be taken for the Printing thereof.
>
> 2. That the Profits . . .[12]

So Dickins and successors reprinted Wesleyana: John Wesley's own works, Charles' hymns, models of piety, Wesley-recommended items. Perhaps most importantly, Dickins published the *Discipline*, year after year, which like the "Large Minutes" really constituted a manual for ministry. Publishing made Wesley's counsel on reading readily available.

The ill-fated Council, Asbury's experiment with centralized governance, devoted considerable attention to publishing and instruction in its two meetings of 1789 and 1790 (see **Appendix**). In its 1789 session, the Council claimed the prerogative "To direct and manage all the Printings which may be done, from Time to Time, for the Use and Benefit of the Methodist Church in *America*." And its 1790 session carried the Council into doing just such direction and managing of Methodist publishing.[13]

So books would be "the answer"? Well, early American Methodism began with somewhat ambiguous guidance on the theological or knowledge dimension of Wesleyan ministerial formation.

The first *Discipline* reiterated word-for-word much of the counsel from the "Large Minutes" on how to "assist those under our Care," to cure the tendency towards Methodist lukewarmness, and to transform a religiosity "not deep, universal, uniform; but superficial, partial, uneven." Repeating Wesley's admonitions, the *Discipline* prescribed caring for both personal and family religion, meeting with members in class, "instructing them in their own Houses," visiting from house to house, and laboring to be skillful "in the work." Both "Large Minutes" and *Discipline* carry the rhetorical protest "This will take up so much Time, that we shall not have Leisure to follow our Studies." The rejoinder, which doubtless salved many a preacher's conscience—

> We answer, 1. Gaining Knowledge is a good Thing, but saving Souls is a better. 2. By this very Thing you will gain the most excellent Knowledge, that of God and Eternity. 3. You will have Time for gaining other Knowledge too. Only sleep not more than you need; and never be idle or triflingly employed. 4. But if you can do but one, let your Studies alone. I would throw by all the Libraries in the world rather than be guilty of the Loss of one Soul.[14]

How often have preachers invoked that as excuse?

Later, of course, the *Discipline* also reiterated Wesley's familiar instructions on "employing our Time" and on how to be both "more *knowing* and more *holy*." With respect to the former, of course, the *Discipline* advised:

16

1. As often as possible to rise at four. 2. From four to five in the Morning, and from five to six in the Evening, to meditate, pray, and read, partly the Scripture with Mr. *Wesley's* Notes, partly the closely-practical Parts of what he has published. 3. From six in the Morning till twelve (allowing an Hour for Breakfast) to read in Order, with much Prayer, *the Christian Library*, and other pious Books.[15]

The *Discipline* then continued with Wesley's insistence that the well-being and rectitude of those "under our Care" and "the Cause of God" depend on our being diligent, never unemployed, never triflingly employed.

"But how?" 1. Read the *most useful* Books, and that regularly and constantly. Steadily spend all the Morning in this Employ, or at least five Hours in four and twenty.

"But I have *no Taste* for Reading." Contract a Taste for it by Use, or return to your Trade.

"But I have no Books." We desire the Assistants will take Care that all the large Societies provide Mr. *Wesley's* Works for the Use of the Preachers.[16]

(I found it interesting that the *Discipline* omitted paragraphs from the "Large Minutes" responding to the query "But I read *only* the *Bible*."[17])

When in 1798, Bishops Thomas Coke and Francis Asbury got around to annotating the *Discipline*, an extraordinarily important expression of early American Methodist theological and ecclesial self-understanding, they devoted a relatively short paragraph to this section, essentially reiterating Wesley's counsel recommending "to our ministers and preachers, agreeably to the directions in this section, *much reading and study*."[18]

Commenting (at greater length) on the section "Of the Duties of those who have the Charge of Circuits," the bishops insist on the importance of reading (and of publishing) for Christian formation, perhaps implicitly thinking of ministerial formation as of that of members. They say:

Next to the preaching of the gospel, the spreading of religious knowledge by the press is of the greatest moment to the people. The soul, whilst united to the body, must be daily fed with pious ideas; otherwise it will lose ground in the divine life. Though the Lord is wonderfully kind to those of his children who are so unfortunate as not to be able to read, yet we are to use all the means in our power. And though the bible be infinitely preferable to all other books, yet we are, even on that very account, to study the writings of those spiritual and great divines, who have by their comments, essays, sermons, or other labours, explained the bible: otherwise, we ought not to attend to the preaching of the gospel; for what is *that* but an explanation and application of the great truths contained in the bible. He, therefore, who has the charge of the circuit, is to be diligent in the sale of those books, which according to the judgment of our conferences and bishops, are deemed profitable for the souls of our people.[19]

Learning by Doing

For the bishops, as perhaps for Wesley, preaching and learning, if in tension over priority and use of time, nevertheless went together because preachers were formed for ministry by doing it. In various other places, they speak about formation for ministry, adding three other features to its shaping. No surprise, they put a high premium on experience, on in-the-saddle formation, on learning by doing, our second facet.

For instance, Bishops Coke and Asbury explained why presiding elders need the power to appoint and move preachers, citing the raw eager zeal of the new preachers needing testing in yet different locales.

Another advantage of this office arises from the necessity of changing preachers from circuit to circuit in the intervals of the yearly conferences. Many of the preachers are young in years and gifts; and this must always be the case, more or less, or a fresh supply of travelling preachers in proportion to the necessities of the work could not be procured. These young men, in general, are exceedingly zealous. Their grand *forte* is to awaken souls; and in this view they are highly necessary for the spreading of the gospel. But for some time their gifts cannot be expected to be *various*; and, therefore, half a year at a time, or sometimes even a quarter, may be sufficient for them labour in one circuit: to change them, therefore, from circuit to circuit, in the intervals of the yearly conference, is highly necessary in many instances.[20]

18

In commenting on the office of deacon and after advancing considerable warrant from scripture and tradition, they again affirmed the on-the-job learning:

> This office serves as an excellent probation for that of an elder. No preacher can be eligible to the office of an elder, till he has exercised the office of a deacon for two years, except in the case of missions. For we would wish to shew the utmost attention to the order of elders, and to have the fullest proof of the abilities, grace, and usefulness of those, who shall be, from time to time, proposed for so important an office as that of a presbyter in the church of God. And we judge, that the man who has proved himself a worthy member of our society, and an useful class-leader, exhorter, and local preacher, who has been approved of for two years as a travelling preacher on trial, and has faithfully served in the office of a traveling deacon for at least two years more has offered such proofs of fidelity and piety, as must satisfy every reasonable mind.[21]

Being Nurtured by the Community

The sequence of roles or offices on which the bishops commented represents both another aspect of the learning-by-trial and yet a third dimension of early Methodism's formation processes. The Methodist community as a whole produced and shaped its leadership. The Disciplinary section, "Of the Method of receiving Preachers, and of their Duty," put together Wesley's "Rules of a Helper" and the ministry questions from the "Method . . . in receiving a New Helper."[22] This section received considerable comment. The examination and the now historic questions, the bishops explained, "when drawn out and enlarged upon by the bishops, as they judge necessary... considered will be found to contain in them the whole of Christian and ministerial experience and practice" (see **Appendix**). They continued, noting that "In respect to doctrines, experience, and practice, the preachers will have passed already through various examinations, before they are received into the travelling connection" (see **Appendix**).

The bishops then rehearsed successive stages of the formative processes begun when converts were admitted into the society on a probationary basis. These new Methodists continued on trial for six months. From the members in class some would be recognized as persons "deeply experienced in divine things" and gifted with the ability to preach, both desirable in class leaders. Those with "an extraordinary gift of prayer and some gift for exhortation, are chosen *the exhorters*." Then fifthly, from the exhorters rose the ranks of local preachers, licenses "signed by the presiding elder, and by the quarterly meeting, which is composed of the local preachers, stewards, and leaders of the circuit." That act of collective discernment during the quarterly meeting continued yearly in renewing licenses. And finally, "Out of the local preachers are chosen *the travelling preachers*, of whom those in full connection form the members of our conferences. These must be on trial for two years before they can be received into full connection with the conference, their character being examined at each conference (whether they be present or absent) in respect to morals, grace, gifts and fruit. Nor can they be received upon trial as *travelling preachers*, till they have obtained a recommendation from the quarterly meetings of their respective circuits." (See **Appendix** for whole statement.[23])

The Methodist community or system as a whole—preaching, classes, disciplines, mutual oversight, testimony, the counsel of "mothers-in-Israel,"[24] quarterly meetings, and love feasts—shaped its leadership. And the system moved talent up the ministerial ladder as quickly and as far as character, grace, gifts, and fruit warranted.

The pattern—reading, observing, hearing, being coached and critiqued—can be seen in the longish excerpt from the journal of William Colbert from December 1790 into early 1792 (see **Appendix**, which tracks his ministerial formation including reading but also being examined and mentored). Colbert sometimes noted reading on successive days (perhaps really at nights?). At other times, the journal entries stand some time apart, perhaps because ongoing reading warranted no comment or perhaps because he failed to find the time for it. His reading included the *Arminian Magazine*, John Milton, the Bible, John Wesley, John Fletcher, selections from the classics, and various items of divinity. As important in his formation was his traveling with other preachers, hearing and doubtless reflecting on their preaching, perhaps being counseled on his own efforts—a true seminar of the road (again, see **Appendix**).[25]

Growing in Grace

Formation came then by reading (Wesley's counsel coming via print), by experience, and by communal discernment, encouragement, and support. The latter—discernment and nurture—pertained especially to the fourth aspect of formation for ministry, the growth in grace, piety, character, morals, or spirituality—as the **Appendix** selection from Colbert's journal also illustrates.

Bishops Coke and Asbury dwelt on that fourth aspect at various places, not surprisingly, in their commentary on the section taken over from the "Large Minutes," which was "Of the Trial of those who think they are moved by the Holy Ghost to preach." Remember, 1. "the love of God abiding in them" and "holy in all manner of conversation," 2. "gifts (as well as grace) for the work," 3. "fruit," convincing auditors of sin and effecting conversions. The bishops remarked:

> We have enlarged on the present subject in our notes on the 8th section of this chapter [the one just excerpted above]. Every reader may from hence perceive the care we take in receiving our preachers and ministers. As the presiding elders, or those who have the charge of circuits, are attentive to the examination of the local preachers and exhorters, so the yearly conferences are attentive to the gifts, grace, and usefulness of all travelling preachers and ministers. Nothing will do for us without the *life of God*. Brilliant parts, fine addresses, &c. are to us but tinkling cymbals, when destitute of the power of the Holy Ghost.
>
> At the same time we are far from despising *talents*, which may be rendered useful to the church of Christ. We know the worth of improved abilities: and nothing can equal our itinerant plan, in the opportunity it affords of suiting our various societies with men of God, who are endued with gifts agreeable to their respective wants.[26]

Yet for all its systemic and communal aspect and as the excerpt from Colbert's journal indicates, formation remained individualistic.[27] The person, the member, preacher-to-be, or preacher read on his own, learned by doing, certainly gained from counsel but individually stood on trial before the group (successively the class, quarterly meeting, and conference.) The technical term for candidacy, still in use when I came through, was "on trial."

21

New converts, as the bishops noted, remained "on trial for six months." But the class meeting and Methodist disciplines put members continually on trial. And the renewing of licenses of the various local officers—stewards, class leaders, exhorters, local preachers—constituted a kind of trial. The stages into full connection constituted, then as now, real trials.

Full members, moreover, continued in a class-like trial. Termed the review of character, it was a mandated feature for every preacher in every annual conference. So American Methodism ritualized annual trials of preachers in the effort to discern spiritual depth, or "grace," along with gifts and fruit, in the individual (in his solitariness). The minutes for the 1785 Conference added the formational question that continues to this day, albeit then as a vital disciplinary factor not an empty ritual. "Question 11. *Are there any objections to any of the preachers? They have been examined one by one.*" By 1787 that had been nuanced to ask, "Question 9. *Are all the preachers blameless in life and conversation?*" They were all strictly tried, one by one, before the Conference.[28]

Through much of the nineteenth century, the review of character retained its class-like rigor. Methodism's premier mid-century historian/interpreter, Abel Stevens explained:

A usage exists in Methodist Conferences, which is without a parallel, we believe, in any other ecclesiastical body. Every member, however venerable with piety and long service, is annually subjected to a sort of judicial examination; put under a virtual arrest, even though there may not be an intimation against his character. No exception is admitted, save that of the presiding officer, who is tried, in a similar manner, at the General Conference. The member thus under examination must stand frankly before all his assembled brethren, any and all of whom may question him, or animadvert on his conduct. His faults, or even mannerisms, are deemed proper subjects of comment, and brotherly counsel; if they amount to vices, the inquiry is converted into a formal trial, and adjudicated according to the laws of the church. This is a severe discipline, and might seem oppressive; but it is self-imposed, it has the sanction of primitive usage, it gives a peculiar confidence, and even tenderness, to the mutual relations of Methodist preachers, and has been very salutary in preserving the purity of the ministry.[29]

Two entries in the minutes of the New England Conference reinforce Stevens's explanation:

> After an excellent and refreshing prayer-meeting of an hour, the Conference resumed its <u>business</u>—that is to say, the examination into the character sustained by every minister connected with the body, which is <u>the</u> work of an annual Methodist Conference, <u>par excellence</u>. Till this is done, the Conference cannot adjourn; and its presiding bishop is subject to arraignment for maladministration, if he fails to "call the name, or cause to be called, that of every preacher . . ."

In 1872 the secretary for that conference, noted in the minutes, with respect to the examination of character, "Then came the fiery ordeal, to which every member of the body must be annually subjected, for all the years of his ecclesiastical life in the Methodist communion, . . ." and reported one complaint referred to "a committee of fifteen for trial."[30]

Another class-like aspect of some conferences, not apparently made routine by inclusion in the *Discipline* or minutes, was the invitation for members to share their experience, to relate their spiritual journey. Early conferences of the United Brethren exhibit that (see **Appendix** for an excerpt), but Methodist conferences occasionally also included such testimony. Coke's notation suggests that it was an American addition to conference practice.

> At each of our Conferences, before we parted, every Preacher gave an account of his experience from the first strivings of the Spirit of God, as far as he could remember; and also of his call to preach, and the success the Lord had given to his labours. It was quite new, but was made a blessing, I am persuaded, to us all.[31]

So preachers, like everyone else, remained on trial, their spiritual journeying as well their continued effectiveness (fruit) and gifts for ministry being regularly assessed.

This first stage of formation then had four aspects, ones that remain important and to which I return as we think about the present:

- Living into Wesley's counsel as set forth in the "Large Minutes" and its later form as the *Discipline*,
- Learning ministry by doing it,
- Being birthed into ministry and nurtured by the Methodist movement as a system,
- Growing spiritually in one's gifts, grace, and fruit.

Looking back at early Methodism, Daniel Curry (president of Indiana Asbury University and later a prominent MEC editor) observed, "The Methodist itinerancy has always been a school as well as a service; though in those early times its facilities for self-culture were as imperfect as were its other appliances."[32]

---

[9] *Minutes of the Annual Conferences of the Methodist Episcopal Church, for the years 1773–1828* (New York: T. Mason and G. Lane for the Methodist Episcopal Church, 1840), referenced as *Minutes*/MEC 1773, 5. This short form of notation standardizes reference to journals of General Conference and books of discipline as well and as variously titled. So *Discipline*/church (in this case The Methodist Episcopal Church or MEC) and the date. A reference to the *Discipline* of the United Methodist Church for 2008 would be cited; e.g., *Discipline*/UMC 2008.

[10] *Minutes*/MEC 1781, 14. Emphasis mine.

[11] On the evolution of the office of book agent and especially the role of John Dickins, in or around 1783 when made publisher, see James P. Pilkington, *The Methodist Publishing House: A History*, 2 vols. (Nashville: Abingdon, 1968, 1989), 1:43–116. (The second volume adds "United" to the title and is authored by Walter Newton Vernon, Jr.)

[12] *Discipline*/MEC 1787, 44.

[13] *Proceedings of the Bishop and Presiding Elders of the Methodist-Episcopal Church, in Council Assembled, at Baltimore, on the First Day of December, 1789* (Baltimore: William Woodard and James Angell, 1789). 3–7. *Minutes; Taken at a Council of the Bishop and Delegated Elders of the Methodist-Episcopal Church: Held at Baltimore in the State of Maryland, December 1, 1790* (Baltimore: W. Goddard and J. Angell, 1790), 3–8.

[14] *Minutes of Several Conversations Between The Rev. Thomas Coke, LL.D. The Rev. Francis Asbury and Others . . . Composing a Form of Discipline* (Philadelphia, 1785), referenced as per above as *Discipline*/MEC 1785, 6–8. For comparison of the "Large" Minutes and first *Discipline* see Jno. J. Tigert, *A Constitutional History of American Episcopal Methodism*, 3rd ed., revised and enlarged (Nashville: Publishing House of the Methodist Episcopal Church, South, 1908), Appendix VII, 532–602, and specifically 538–42.

[15] *Discipline*/MEC 1785, 18. Instead of "other pious Books," the "Large Minutes" specified the Wesleyan piety needed, namely "the other Books which we have published in prose and verse."

[16] *Discipline*/MEC 1785, 18–19.

[17] Tigert, *Constitutional History*, 563.

[18] Thomas Coke and Francis Asbury, *The Doctrines and Disciplines of the Methodist Episcopal Church, in America* (Philadelphia: Henry Tuckniss, 1798), 107.

[19] Coke and Asbury, *Doctrines and Discipline* (1798), 77–78.

[20] Ibid. 50.

[21] Ibid. 57.

[22] See Tigert, *A Constitutional History*, 550–51; 579–80.

[23] Coke and Asbury, *Doctrines and Discipline* (1798), 66–67.

[24] See the Appendix for an instance of the formative spiritual direction and perhaps two mother-in-Israel relationships described by Henry Boehm in J. B. Wakeley, *The Patriarch of One Hundred Years: Being Reminiscences, Historical and Biographical, of Rev. Henry Boehm* (New York: Nelson & Phillips, 1875); facsimile reprint, Abram W. Sangrey, ed. (Lancaster 1982), 60–61.

[25] *A Journal of the Travels of William Colbert, Methodist Preacher: thro' parts of Maryland, Pennsylvania, New York, Delaware and Virginia in 1790 to 1838* (10 volume typescript, used at Drew) 1: 26, 27, 28, 32, 36–37, 39, 40, 41, 55, 73, 74, 77.

[26] Coke and Asbury, *Doctrines and Discipline* (1798), 83–84.

[27] "Until the year 1816 the theological training of the Methodist ministry, a training largely *doctrinal*, was left to the discretion of the individual, a discretion educated by Methodist tradition, enlivened by the demands of the discipline, and strengthened by the example and expectation of the founders of the Church and their early successors. No set group of studies was outlined, no formal examination upon prescribed books held, no special helps for directing the study of young ministers were afforded, and no pecuniary assistance in purchasing books given by the Church." Elmer Guy Cutshall, "The Doctrinal Training of the Traveling Ministry of the Methodist Episcopal church," Ph.D. University of Chicago, 1922, 24.

[28] *Minutes/MEC 1785*, 23; *Minutes/1787*, 27.

[29] Abel Stevens, *Memorials of the Early Progress of Methodism in the Eastern States,* 2nd Series (New York: Carlton & Phillips, 1854), 39.

[30] *Minutes of the New England Conference of the Methodist Episcopal Church ... 1868*, 8–9; *Minutes of the New England Conference of the Methodist Episcopal Church ... 1872*, 5, 6.

[31] Thomas Coke, *Extracts of the Journals of the Rev. Dr. Coke's Five Visits to America* (London, Printed by G. Paramore; and sold by G. Whitfield, 1793), 151. For the UB pattern see Russell E. Richey, Kenneth E. Rowe, and Jean Miller Schmidt, *The Methodist Experience in America: A Sourcebook* (Nashville: Abingdon Press, 2000), 1800b.

[32] Daniel Curry, "Life and Times of Bishop Hedding," *Methodist Quarterly Review* 37 (1855), Fourth series 7, 589–614, 599. Curry was writing about Hedding around 1801 and concerning the New York Conference.

Collegial
Yokefellowed Tutelage

Although Bishops Coke and Asbury did not find reason to mention the practice explicitly, by the 1790s Methodism often exercised ministry and cared for ministerial formation by appointing two persons to a circuit. The bishops acknowledged the supervisory and tutoring role implicitly as they commented in "Of the Duties of those who have the Charge of Circuits." They put first among the duties that of supervising those learning by trial:

> The person who holds it [the circuit] is to watch over the other travelling preachers in his circuit, not with the eye of severe judge, but with that of a tender elder brother. He should indeed be faithful to his colleagues and tell them all their faults; but he has no power to correct them. He is to bear an equal share with them in the toils of a travelling preacher, besides having upon him the care of all the churches in his circuit. But if his colleagues will not observe his reasonable direction or behave grossly amiss, he must inform his presiding elder, whose duty it is, as soon as possible, to judge of and rectify every thing.[33]

By the time the bishops penned this, they and American Methodism had developed the practice of appointing two preachers to a circuit, routinely putting a young or junior under the senior preacher in charge, and thereby formalizing apprenticeships in ministry.

Journals speak of being appointed, of so-and-so being "my colleague." Sometimes the two spoke of and were spoken of as "yokefellows."[34]

Would they have thought of themselves as like the seventy Jesus appointed (Luke 10:1-12, 17-20) and sent out ahead of him, "two by two, into every town and place where he was to come," as the "Lord's few laborers sent out into his harvest," indeed even "as lambs in the midst of wolves"? Better equipped than the seventy, Methodist itinerants boasted at least a horse and saddlebags with a Bible, *Discipline*, and hymnal.

Two-by-two was so normative that when an appointment lacked a colleague, the preachers' journals remark on that fact. So their journals indicated that the occasional solitary appointment was not a typical or welcome event.

Tutor, Mentor, Supervisor

Theological education gained then a new agent—tutor, mentor, supervisor—adding a semi-official instructor to the community's guidance, strengthening that particular formational element of the four Wesley identified as desired. William McKendree noted:

> In 1788, I was appointed to Mecklenburg Circuit. This was a fortunate station for me. Mr. Cox, with whom I was appointed to travel, was an instructor and father to me. The old professors knew how to sympathize with young preachers. It looked to me like they wished to bear a part of the cross for me. In this circuit there were many deeply experienced Christians, by whose walk and conversation I profited much. I hope I shall never forget how sweetly they used to talk of the triumphs of grace and the love of Jesus. After a sufficient trial, I expected the preachers would be convinced that I never would make a profitable preacher; that I should by that means returns to the comforts that I had left behind. But the year rolled round, and I was "continued on trial." The dear people seemed unwilling to part with me, for we had spent some sweet moments together.[35]

Moving those on trial to a new circuit often, typically yearly, meant that they enjoyed mentoring from and apprenticeship under various senior preachers. McKendree reported:

In 1790, I was appointed to travel with Jesse Nicholson, on Portsmouth Circuit; but was removed, and spent the latter part of the year with William Spencer, on Surry Circuit. This was a year of much comfort to my soul. I found an affectionate people indeed: many were deeply experienced saints, who were a blessing to me. "As iron sharpeneth iron," so did the conversation of those brethren provoke me to love and good works. I found father, mother, brother, and sister, indeed and in truth. It was my meat and drink to employ my spare moments in study. Fasting and prayer was a pleasure. I had an almost uninterrupted heaven below. The work of the Lord prospered in our hands, particularly in the latter part of the year. A considerable number of members was added to the societies.[36]

A compilation of the appointments on a Baltimore Conference circuit from 1774 to 1837 well illustrates the diverse mentoring of junior by senior preachers. Two persons were assigned to this circuit from the beginning. Until 1811 preachers in charge changed every year. In 1810 and 1811 the junior colleague on the circuit returned and that occurred again a decade later. But, with those exceptions, for a half century the junior on that circuit changed yearly.[37] That guaranteed those on trial, the junior itinerants, a succession of mentors and supervisors (and of annually changed learning contexts and communities of formation).

"Family" Ties

This kind of formational yokefellow relationship may be hard to picture, given the image we have of circuit riders, riding alone from appointment to appointment, and half a circuit away from their colleague. However, as I have commented several times elsewhere, colleagues on a circuit and preachers from other circuits found themselves together for a considerable portion of the appointment year. I have several times exhibited this togetherness with another set of extracts from the journals of William Colbert.[38] Itinerants like Colbert rode from conference and to conference with colleague(s), a trip that could take weeks. They labored together at their own quarterly and camp meetings and often at those of neighboring circuits. And they doubtless found it necessary to be together for other events. Colleague preachers together at quarterly conferences, on the road to and from such events, and in the evenings may have spent more sustained and intimate time together than many clergy now do with their spouses.

The relationship between the two appointed to a circuit, at times, approximated familial ties as Nathan Bangs, Methodism's first great historian, indicated in a semi-centennial sermon:

> In mentioning Canada, my mind is carried back to the time when the Lord "took my feet out of the horrible pit and miry clay," and "put a new song into my mouth," in the month of May, 1800. From this happy period of my life, God has dealt very mercifully with me, in leading me in a way I had not before known. In the month of September, 1801, I was induced, through much fear and trembling, to enter upon the travelling ministry, under the presiding eldership of the Rev. Joseph Jewel, and as a colleague with my spiritual father, the Rev. Joseph Sawyer.[39]

The appellation "father," applied later and commonly to older members of the itinerancy as an honorific title, also pointed to the special paternal roles they had exercised, typically for more than one member of a conference.[40]

One such mentoring, apprenticeship relationship, exhibited in their journals by both parties, was remarkable for its reciprocity. Dan Young reported:

> The following year (1806) I was sent to Barre Circuit, in Vermont. This to me was a memorable year. I had for my senior preacher that excellent and distinguished man of God, Elijah Hedding. I am sure I never saw a more worthy man. I was intimately acquainted with him for many years, and I know not that I ever saw anything in him that would have been inconsistent in St. Paul. An attachment had existed between us before we met in our work on the circuit, and when we met, it very soon matured into warmest friendship and Christian love. He often remarked that our love was like to that of David and Jonathan. At the commencement of our work we entered into a mutual agreement to tell each other of all the errors and improprieties that we knew, saw, or heard of each other. This agreement was

faithfully kept, to the advantage of both. We so arranged the circuit as to be often together at our meetings, in which we preached alternately. The one who heard watched and noted all the errors of the one speaking, and gave him a faithful account of them. This was a great means of improvement. "We had not labored long till a gradual but good work of God broke out nearly all round the circuit, which continued throughout the year."[41]

Virtually reiterating this account for 1806 (see **Appendix**), the biographer for the young, later-bishop Hedding, reported as well on the collegial relationships that had been formational for Hedding.

Reason for Growth

Peter Cartwright, with typical bluster, championed the yoked program of theological formation as superior to any other and the reason for Methodism's explosive growth. He recalled that his presiding elder, William McKendree "directed me to a proper course of reading and study. He selected books for me, both literary and theological; and every quarterly visit he made, he examined into my progress, and corrected my errors, if I had fallen into any. He delighted to instruct me in English grammar." He continued, "My business was to preach, meet the classes, visit the society and the sick, and then to my books and study; and I say that I am more indebted to Bishop M'Kendree for my little attainments in literature and divinity, than to any other man on earth. And I believe that if presiding elders would do their duty by young men in this way, it would be more advantageous than all the colleges and Biblical institutes in the land; for they then could learn and practice every day." (See **Appendix** for this selection.)

Cartwright then contrasted this system and its production of the dramatic growth of American Methodism with the languishing of British Methodism and the poor performance of American denominations that also contended "for an educated ministry, for pews, for instrumental music, for a congregational or stated salaried ministry." With respect to the latter—the "Presbyterians and other Calvinistic branches of the Protestant Church"—and their formal educational requirements for ministry and heightened ministerial expectations, Cartwright asserted, "The Methodists universally opposed these ideas; and the illiterate Methodist preachers actually set the world on fire [the American world, at least] while they were lighting their matches!"[42]

Cartwright indicated that his ministerial formation occurred before the introduction of the course of study, the next phase to which we attend. It too presumed continuation of the two older patterns, the fourfold dimension of the Wesleyan **Counseled** and the yoked relationships of the **Collegial** that Cartwright touted.[43]

---

[33] Coke and Asbury, *Doctrines and Discipline* (1798), 72.

[34] "There was another local preacher . . . . And we were as true yoke fellows in the gospel and labored together." David L. Steele, ed., "The Autobiography of the Reverend John Young, 1747–1837," *Methodist History* 13 (Oct. 1974), 17–40, 31. On this stage of ministerial formation see Frederick V. Mills, Sr. "Mentors of Methodism, 1784–1844," *Methodist History* 12 (Oct. 1973), 43–57. See references to colleague, co-laborer, and yokefellow in J. W. Hedges, comp., *Crowned Victors: The Memoirs of Over Four Hundred Methodist Preachers, Including the First Two Hundred and Fifty Who Died on This Continent,* "Introduction" by A. E. Gibson (Baltimore: Methodist Episcopal Book Depository, 1878).

[35] Robert Paine, *Life and Times of William M'Kendree, Bishop of the Methodist Episcopal Church,* 2 vols. (Nashville: Publishing House of the Methodist Episcopal, South, 1874), 1: 57–58. See the Appendix for Paine's characterization of this relationship and mention of the relationship as well to James O'Kelly in whose schism McKendree briefly participated.

[36] Ibid. 1:60.

[37] J. H. Young, "Sketches of Methodism: Its Rise and Progress on Montgomery Circuit, Baltimore Conference," *The Methodist Magazine* 20 (1838), new series # 9, 215–27, 222–23.

[38] See Russell E. Richey, *Marks of Methodism: Theology in Ecclesial Practice,* United Methodism and American Culture 5 (Nashville: Abingdon Press, 2005), 44–46.

[39] Nathan Bangs, *A Semi-Centennial Sermon, Delivered at the Request of and Before the New-York East Conference, June 12, 1852.* Published by Order of the Conference (New York: Carlton & Phillips, 1852), 5.

[40] See James B. Finley, *Sketches of Western Methodism: Biographical, Historical, and Miscellaneous. Illustrative of Pioneer Life,* ed. W. P. Strickland (Cincinnati: Printed at the Book Concern, 1857), 6, 59, 61, 94, 100, 176, 183, 243–44, 328, 332, 337, 431, 481 for mention of fathers, Walker, Ragin, Rankins, Walker, Ellis, Kobler, Lakin, Axley, Brown, Collins, Emory, and Taylor—first names not needed. Similarly in W. P. Strickland, *The Life of Jacob Gruber* (New York: Carlton & Porter, 1860), see references to fathers Turck, Richards, Howe, Ware, Abbott, and Gruber, pp. 9, 24, 298, 299, 355.

[41] W. P. Strickland, ed., *Autobiography of Dan Young, A New England Preacher of the Olden Time* (New York: Carlton & Porter, 1860), 47–48 (see Appendix for the account from Elijah Hedding's side).

[42] Peter Cartwright, *Autobiography of Peter Cartwright: The Backwoods Preacher,* ed. W. P. Strickland (New York: Carlton & Porter, 1857), 78–79.

[43] The passing of the circuit as a system for theological education was noted in the late nineteenth century. See the Appendix for the import of the change in William F. Warren, "Ministerial Education in Our Church," *Methodist Quarterly Review* 54 (1872): 246–67, 253.

Conferenced

Course of Study Guidance and Accountability

N ot everyone shared Cartwright's judgment that apprenticed, collegial, circuit-riding formation delivered fully and adequately. In 1815, Joseph Trimble, serving as president pro tempore of the New England Conference "addressed the Conference concerning the necessity of Preachers being diligent in their Studies and Labors."[44] The next year, the 1816 General Conference, in something of a crisis mood after the death en route of Bishop Asbury, heard from its "committee of *ways and means*, appointed to provide a more ample support of the ministry among us, to prevent locations, and the admission of improper persons into the itinerancy."

All three factors—ministerial salaries, locations, and scrounging for replacements—the committee indicated materially reduced the intellectual caliber of the itinerancy. Inadequate salary led many of the most able to "locate" and thus necessitated the admission of those insufficiently gifted or prepared—"obliging us to fill up the vacancies with persons not competent to the work assigned them." The committee then affirmed:

Although a collegiate education is not, by your committee, deemed essential to a gospel ministry, yet it appears absolutely necessary for every minister of the gospel to study to show himself approved unto God, a workman that needeth not to be ashamed. Every one, therefore, who would be useful as a minister in the Church, should, to a sincere piety and laudable zeal for the salvation of souls, add an ardent desire for useful knowledge—he should strive by every lawful means to imbue his mind with every science which is intimately connected with the doctrine of salvation by Jesus Christ, and which will enable him to understand and illustrate the sacred Scriptures.[45]

Study to Show Thyself Approved

The committee prescribed and General Conference embraced a series of remedies. The seventh was to assign to the bishops "or a committee which they may appoint in each annual conference" the duty of pointing out "a course of reading and study proper to be pursued by candidates for the ministry" and provision for an examination on the recommended subjects.[46] Nathan Bangs, who reproduced the whole report, then observed: "From that time forth a regular course of study has been prescribed by the bishops for those on trial in the annual conferences, to which the candidates must attend, and give satisfactory evidence of their attainments, especially in theological science, before they can be admitted into full membership as itinerant ministers." He conceded, however, that initially the course was "very limited in some of the conferences and the examinations comparatively superficial."[47]

So annual conferences assumed responsibility for theological content in ministerial preparation and for monitoring the two-year reading course. Conferences (with the bishops) became the educational system, setting the curriculum, enriching the apprenticeship to include explicit attention to the reading program, monitoring individuals' progress each year at the annual gathering, and certifying completion and theological adequacy.[48]

In 1817, the Baltimore Conference addressed the General Conference mandate. It framed the reading biblically and doctrinally:

The Holy Ghost saith, "Study to shew thyself approved unto God, a workman that needeth not be ashamed: right dividing the word of Truth"— To this end the preacher should be sufficiently acquainted with the depravity of the human heart—Redemption by Christ—Re-

34

pentance towards God—Justification by faith in our Lord Jesus Christ, who is very and Eternal God—The direct Witness of the Spirit—Holiness of heart and Life, and also the doctrine of Perseverance—The Resurrection of the dead and future Rewards and Punishments.

To enforce these doctrines with propriety, the teacher must be conversant with Scriptures in general, and with Geography and History.

The art of conveying ideas with ease, propriety and clearness is of great importance. The Candidate should understand the Articles of Religion, and the doctrines and discipline of the Church, to which he is to subscribe, and by which he is to be governed.

1st On Divinity, a constant use of the Holy Scriptures. Wesley's Sermons—Notes—answer to Taylor—Saints Rest—Law's Serious Call—Benson's Sermons—Coke's Commentaries—Fletcher's Checks—Appeal—Portrait of Saint Paul—Wood's Dictionary—Newton on the Prophecies—and Wesley's Philosophy.

2nd Rollins' Ancient History, Josephus's Antiquities, with Wesley's Ecclesiastical History.

3rd. The Rudiments of the English language, Alexander's, Murray's, or Webster's Grammar.

4th. Morse's Universal and Paine's Geography.[49]

The points of doctrine and list of books grew gradually over the years. The list offered the Indiana Conference by Bishops R. R. Roberts and Joshua Soule at its 1832 organizing sessions added to the areas of knowledge and included Richard Watson's *Theological Institutes*, Johann Mosheim's *Ecclesiastical History*, Thomas Reid's *Philosophy*, William Paley's *Natural Theology* and *Evidences of Christianity*, Isaac Watts's *Logic*, and the *Methodist Magazine*.[50]

Authorized (Not Mandated), Limited and Partial

Perhaps La Roy Sunderland had this particular course in view when two years later he trashed Methodist practices of formation in general and the course of study in particular (see **Appendix**). He complained that the *Discipline* authorized rather than mandated the course, that in many places "nothing is done," and that the disuse included his own conference. "Lately," he conceded, "in the South Carolina,

Philadelphia, Mississippi, Alabama, and Georgia conferences, a uniform system of study has been adopted, which candidates for deacon's and elder's orders are required to pursue; and according to which they are to be examined, it seems, once a year for four years successively. A similar course had been prepared and printed by a committee of the New-York conference, and approved of by the bishops, which has been used with good effect, I am informed, in that conference."

Sunderland also had doubts about the by then standard and traditional pattern of formation-in-the-saddle. "The persons for whom these plans for study are recommended, it must be remembered, have already commenced the multifarious and arduous duties of the Gospel ministry, without any considerable knowledge of theology, and sometimes, perhaps, without any kind of an education whatever; so that about all they know, both of letters and divinity, they must pick up, after they have engaged in their pastoral labors—labors, which, under any circumstances, are enough, as every faithful minister knows, to require all the lime, and patience, and attention, which any one can bestow."[51]

Viewing the course as limited and partial "considering the nature of the sacred office" and finding on the course just seven books in biblical and systematic theology, he thundered, "[I]n all seven different works! And are these thought sufficient to give a student a competent knowledge of the science of interpreting the Bible? A sufficient knowledge of Christian theology for a public teacher of religion, to be derived from some half a dozen books!" Sunderland—on leave as an anti-slavery activist, soon to be editor of *Zion's Watchman*, and among the founders of the Wesleyan Methodist Church—was just getting warmed up.[52] "In the above course, it will be perceived, two of the most important branches of theological study are nearly, if not entirely, omitted; those branches which are most generally called 'exegetical,' and 'practical theology.'" How, he wondered, would ministers gain the critical and interpretive knowledge that would permit them to "arrive at the true sense and meaning taught in the Bible, and by which he may interpret this Book for *himself?*" The want of schooling in practical theology, including especially "every thing relating to the theory of sacred eloquence, and the performance of every duty connected with the care of souls," he thought equally dire (see **Appendix**).[53]

36

Sunderland concluded with an exhortation that, one might suggest, had already been voiced and heard by others, namely that the Methodist Episcopal Church needed "to do her part toward evangelizing the world" and to the Christianization of "these United States." For this, the MEC's mission (reforming the continent and spreading scriptural holiness over these lands) "she must advance in the education of her ministers. . . . This is a new country; the moral and intellectual habits of the people are yet, in no small degree, to be formed. This must be done by education, by sanctified learning. . . . Those ministers who take the lead in promoting the means and blessings of sanctified learning will wield the future destinies of this powerful nation."[54]

The same year, George Peck a future editor of the *Methodist Quarterly Review* and then principal of Cazenovia Seminary, offered a similar critique of Methodism's system of preparing its ministers and specifically of the course of study. He thought they began too low, lacked suitable texts, and jumbled those on the course "without much classification or order." The exam, covering the whole course, produced "such a terrible siege" that some withdraw and others, in fright, "are not able to answer questions which are at other times perfectly familiar to them."[55] (Thankfully nothing like that happens today.)

The course of study did not wither under Sunderland's and Peck's blistering attacks. As we will see in our treatment of other ministerial formational stages, Methodism worked steadily to refine, elaborate, and improve the course—often in response to just such critiques. It later developed conference schools to reinforce its pedagogy, and outlined separate courses for each and every ministerial office and language conference. And, of course, course of study continues to this very day.

Further, as Methodism—over the middle decades of the nineteenth century—settled into small towns and cities, it deployed more and more of its ministry in station appointments. Effectively gone, thereby, were the circuit, the yoked appointment of senior and junior itinerant, and the apprenticeship system that had given some level of supervision to the earlier styles of Methodist formational processes (see just such a judgment by William Warren in the **Appendix**).

[44] *Minutes of the New England Conference of the Methodist Episcopal Church . . .1766 to . . . 1845*, 2 vols. (Typescript prepared by George Whitaker for New England Methodist Historical Society, 1912), 1:215 (1815).

[45] Nathan Bangs, *A History of the Methodist Episcopal Church*, 8th ed., 4 vols. (New York: Carlton & Porter, 1860) 3:43–44. Bangs reproduced the whole report of the committee of ways and means.

[46] Ibid., 47.

[47] Ibid., 48. On the course of study, see L. Dale Patterson, "The Ministerial Mind of American Methodism: The Course of Study for the Ministry of the Methodist Episcopal Church, the Methodist Episcopal Church, South and the Methodist Protestant Church, 1876–1920," Ph.D. Dissertation, Drew University.

[48] On the ministerial style in this period, see E. Brooks Holifield, *God's Ambassadors: A History of the Christian Clergy in America* (Grand Rapids and Cambridge: William B. Eerdmans Publishing Company, 2007), 124–26.

[49] Baltimore Conference Journal, Ms., 1817, 99–100; quoted by William J. E. Apsley, "The Educational Concerns, 1816–61," in *Those Incredible Methodists: A History of the Baltimore Conference of the United Methodist Church*, Gordon Pratt Baker, ed. (Baltimore: Commission on Archives and History, Baltimore Conference, 1972), 132–33.

[50] William Warren Sweet, *Circuit-rider Days in Indiana* (Indianapolis: W. K. Stewart Co., 1916), 107–08.

[51] La Roy Sunderland, "Essay on a Theological Education," "Written by request of the Junior Preachers' Society of the New England Conference by Rev. La Roy Sunderland, Member of the said Conference." *The Methodist Magazine* 16 (1834, new series #5), 423–37, 430.

[52] See short biography in James E. Kirby, Russell E. Richey and Kenneth E. Rowe, *The Methodists*, Denominations in America 8 (Westport, CT, and London: Greenwood Press, 1996), 358–60.

[53] Sunderland, "Essay on a Theological Education," 431.

[54] Ibid. 437.

[55] George Peck, "An Address Delivered Before the Literary Society of the Oneida Conference, September 28, 1834," *The Methodist Magazine and Quarterly Review* 18 (1836, new series #7), 47–69, 63–64. For an illustration of such sporadic reading, see the citations from the journal of Jacob Lanius in Richey, *Doctrine in Experience*, 146–47. Lanius effectively quit mentioning reading once he was ordained elder.

Collegiate

Formation in Class and Chapel

I n his vision for the future stated in his 1834 "Essay on Theological Education," La Roy Sunderland cleverly did not indicate explicitly whether he thought this education for ministry could be accomplished in colleges or required Methodism to found theological seminaries (though by using "theological education" in the title he let imaginations run and prompted multiple critiques in the *Methodist Magazine* the next year). However, he, like George Peck, voiced sentiments and offered remedies prescribed, over a decade earlier, by the 1820 General Conference, recommendations that gradually led to collegiate institutions. A committee, chaired by Nathan Bangs, had proposed that the MEC establish its own education institutions.

> Almost all seminaries [academies and colleges] of learning in our country, of much celebrity, are under the control of Calvinistic or of Hopkinsian principles, or otherwise are managed by men denying the fundamental doctrines of the gospel. If any of our people, therefore, wish to give their sons or daughters a finished education, they are under the necessity of resigning them to the management of those institutions that are more or less hostile to our views of the grand doctrines of Christianity.
>
> Another capital defect in most seminaries of learning, your committee presumes to think, is that experimental and practical god-

liness is considered only of secondary importance; whereas, in the opinion of your committee, this ought to form the most prominent feature in every literary institution. Religion and learning should mutually assist each other, and thus connect the happiness of both worlds together.

General Conference then recommended that "all the annual conferences" establish "as soon as practicable literary institutions under their own control" and ordered that "a copy of this report be recorded on the journals of the several Annual Conferences."[56]

Kentucky and Ohio Conferences collaborated to establish Augusta College in 1822, but conferences really rallied to the collegiate cause in the 1830s: Randolph Macon in 1830, Wesleyan University (Connecticut), Dickinson and Allegheny in 1833, and Emory and two women's colleges—Wesleyan College (Georgia) and Greensboro in 1836. Other collegiate establishments followed quickly, some two hundred by the Civil War. Most however were poorly funded, staffed, supported, and attended, and consequently did not long survive. Some thirty-four did,[57] primarily because the supporting conferences made education their highest priority. So the minutes of the early sessions of the North Carolina Conference attest, various supportive, infrastructural, and staffing matters dominating their first four yearly gatherings.[58]

To Educate Their Own

Methodism went into the college-founding binge, out of both aspiration and desperation. By the 1830s and 1840s, leaders began to claim their church's role in the molding of a Christian America. They also recognized as a crisis what the Bangs committee had forewarned in 1820: If Methodism did not educate its own, its talented youth would resort to the private and public universities dominated by the Calvinists (Presbyterians and Congregationalists), be seduced into fatal heresy, and be lost. So insisted Stephen Olin, president of Wesleyan in 1844, sounding a then common refrain:

No Christian denomination can safely trust to others for the training of its sons. . . . History has too clearly demonstrated that, without colleges of our own, few of our sons are likely to be educated, and that only a small portion of that few are likely to be retained in our communion.

He estimated that three-quarters of the Methodists who had attended others' college had been "lost":

Many of them have gone to other denominations; many more have gone to the world. All were the legitimate children of the Church. They were her hope, and they should have become the crown of her rejoicing.[59]

When, however, founders came to articulate the aims of the new colleges and to envision their curricula, they stressed that the schools would offer a classical education, would be open to persons of various faiths, and would be non-sectarian. Ministerial formation, then, did not figure prominently in the public self-presentation of the schools, but it motivated intradenominational rationale and then shaped the school's program, ethos, sponsorship, faculty, and student body. "Such an Institution," wrote one of Methodism's educators concerning Wesleyan University, "will give a character & influence to our Church, . . . will gradually improve the taste & talents of our Ministry and add to their weight and influence in society at large."[60]

The colleges constituted the Methodist "seminaries" of the day. Of Randolph Macon's 210 early graduates,

48 became teachers, thirteen of whom taught in one of the church's colleges
43 became ministers, twelve of whom served at one point or another on a faculty or as president of school
39 became lawyers, eight of whom became legislators
29 became physicians
39 returned to farming.[61]

Of Wesleyan University's first forty years of graduates (919), a third entered the Methodist ministry and according to Duvall, Wesleyan produced three-quarters of the ministers who had college degrees.[62]

41

Formed for Ministry

The seminary-like aspect of collegiate education is well illustrated in the letters and journal of Isaac Jennison, a Wesleyan University student, 1837–41 (see **Appendix**). Of his fellow students, Jennison wrote his parents, "It is an interesting sight to behold such a number of young men as are here assembled, sixty or more of whom are members of the Methodist E. Church, and a great part of whom are preparing to preach the everlasting gospel." His daily regimen, doubtless one that John Wesley would have blessed, had a monastic aspect:

> I have no time to lose—have employment for every moment. We attend prayers in the morning at six o'clock, in the chapel, immediately after which we repair to our respective recitation rooms; thence to breakfast; return to our rooms, and study until eleven, when we recite again; dine at twelve; exercise and study until five, P. M., when we have prayers again in the chapel; retire at ten in the evening; and thus passes the day, with other exercises which occur in their proper place. . . .

He kept his parents informed about "Sabbath" services, revivals, and other religiously formative experiences. "I find," he reported, "that college is no place for idleness, but a place for application and constant effort. I have joined the society termed the Missionary Lyceum. Last evening attended love-feast in the chapel—it was a good season. This day has nearly gone: how fast time flies! It is constantly bearing me to the tomb. May I wisely improve the passing privileges!"

Although he left campus for services, he had ample spiritual opportunities over a typical Wesleyan week.

> Sabbath, A. M., meeting in the college chapel, when either Dr. Fisk, or the chaplain. Rev. Prof. Holdich, preaches. In the afternoon attend church in the city, in the place of regular circuit preaching. At half-past five of the same day we have a prayer meeting in some one of the rooms of college. Wednesday evening, class meeting; Friday evening, prayer meeting; Saturday evening, band meeting, which to me, and I may say to all who attend, is the most profitable exercise. This evening have been much blessed in band.[63]

Later entries documented the hold on Wesleyan of holiness doctrines, the regular campus revivals, Jennison's own yearning for the gift of holiness of heart, his experience of sanctification in a camp meeting at Bolton, his own preaching and teaching, continued reading of John Fletcher and Phoebe Palmer, daily small group campus meetings at one point for spiritual growth, and his licensing as a local preacher by "the quarterly conference of the Wesleyan University."[64] At several points, he wrote of death or eternity. He met that fate. Jennison died June 11th 1841, just short of his graduation.

Like other Methodist colleges, Wesleyan represented itself as non-sectarian and as offering a classical education, which would equip persons for public life. However, as Jennison's experience indicates, a Methodist faculty, extra-curricular religious activities, regular chapel, and the overall ethos formed many for ministry so oriented and committed.[65]

So by the mid-nineteenth century, the Methodist family of churches had birthed a number of colleges, including, of course my own and my most recent employer (B.A. Wesleyan; employed by Emory University).

Creating colleges fulfilled the primary goal of educating and forming students for Methodist ministry. However, as with many endeavors, the results rippled beyond the original target:

- The colleges did assemble the church's theological leadership.
- They established templates for ministerial formation.
- They produced studies of church and ministry, particularly through the *Methodist Quarterly Review*(s)—for the MEC and the Methodist Episcopal Church, South (MECS).
- Their faculty provided the books that the course of study required candidates to read.
- But scattered as they were, they required any who would attend from any distance to uproot themselves and move to that locale.
- And that latter population would then have to gain their circuit-riding style of formation on their own and/or under some other auspices than that of their own conference.

[56] Bangs, *History*, 3:105–07. The New England Conference dutifully spread the General Conference legislation on its minutes. See *Minutes of the New England Conference of the Methodist Episcopal Church . . . 1766 to . . .1845*, 1: 301–02 (1820). The Ohio Conference apparently did not get the message. See William Warren Sweet, ed. *Circuit-Rider Days Along the Ohio. Being the Journals of the Ohio Conference from its Organization in 1812 to 1826* (New York and Cincinnati: The Methodist Book Concern, 1923), 185–214. Thomas M. Drake turned down an invitation to join the Wesleyan University faculty, explaining that he needed to remain at Ohio University (Athens): "First I was chosen in a storm & contest between Presbyterians & the Friends of Methodism for power in this Institution. . . . I am the only Officer belonging to Our Church in the Institution." He could not leave, he continued, "unless there was some other person to take my place here, who would stand fast for *the best of causes* & protect the concerns of Methodism . . ." Frederick A. Norwood, ed., "More Letters to Laban Clark, Relating Particularly to the History of Wesleyan University," *Methodist History* 11 (Oct. 1972), 30–41, 33–34.

[57] Donald G. Tewksbury, *The Founding of American Colleges and Universities Before the Civil War* (New York: Arno Press & The New York Times, 1969), 103–11. John O. Gross, *Methodist Beginnings in Higher Education* (Nashville: Division of Educational Institutions, Board of Education, The Methodist Church, 1959).

[58] Methodist Episcopal Church, South. N. C. Conference. Minutes of The North Carolina Annual Conference, 1838–1885, 2 vols. Xerox Copy of Original Handwritten Minutes, Duke University, 1: 7b, 8b, 9b–10a, 12a–13a, 25a–26a. Summarized in Richey, *Doctrine in Experience*, 153–54.

[59] "Christian Education," *The Works of Stephen Olin, D. D., LL.D., Late President of the Wesleyan University* (New York: Harper & Brothers, Publishers, 1852), II, 240–53. Citations from 249 and 251.

[60] Thomas Drake, in the letter already cited, though declining the offer to join the Wesleyan faculty, celebrated its formation. Norwood, ed., "More Letters to Laban Clark," *Methodist History* 11 (Oct. 1972), 33.

[61] These figures, from the Society of the Alumni, are reported by James Edward Scanlon, *Randolph-Macon College. A Southern History, 1825–1967* (Charlottesville: University Press of Virginia, 1983).

[62] Slyvanus M. Duvall, *The Methodist Episcopal Church and Education Up to 1869* (New York: Bureau of Publications, Teachers College, 1928) 39–40. For somewhat different assessments see David B. Potts, *Wesleyan University, 1831–1910: Collegiate Enterprise in New England* (New Haven and London: Yale University Press, 1992) and Glenn T. Miller, *Piety and Intellect. The Aims and Purposes of Ante-Bellum Theological Education* (Atlanta: Scholars Press, 1990), 127–39.

[63] Edward Otheman, *The Christian Student. Memoir of Isaac Jennison, Jr. Late a Student of the Wesleyan University, Middletown, Conn. Containing his Biography, Diary, and Letters* (New York: G. Lane & P. P. Sandford for the Methodist Episcopal Church, 1843), 38–43.

[64] Ibid., 189.

[65] On Methodist ministerial formation, the church's colleges, and the launching of theological schools, see Glenn T. Miller, *Piety and Intellect: The Aims and Purposes of Ante-Bellum Theological Education* (Atlanta: Scholars Press, 1990), 303–436; and *Piety and Profession: American Theological Education, 1870–1970* (Grand Rapids and Cambridge: William B. Eerdmans Publishing Company, 2007), 246–70.

Seminary
Specialized Theological Formation

B y the mid-nineteenth century Methodism aspired to exercise leadership in America and in the Protestant campaign to Christianize
America. Given the denomination's size, spread, and prosperity,
some within its ranks began to look favorably on the theological seminaries founded by Congregationalists and Presbyterians, specifically en-
vying the prominence and importance of Andover and Princeton. Some,
like Sunderland, left ambiguous whether theological education required
separate higher educational institutions or could be accomplished in
the church's colleges. Others writing at essentially the same time, like
then *Christian Advocate* editor, John P. Durbin, were more forthright,
urging fellow Methodists to divest themselves "of our prejudices against
theological seminaries."[66] (Durbin's advocacy is interesting since in some
ways he might be deemed the preeminent example of the best outcome
from the traditional formational processes. He had done college *after*
entering the itinerancy, had later joined the Augusta faculty, and soon
after penning the editorial became president of Dickinson.)

Other prominent Methodists joined in advocacy for theological
education, among them James Strong and Randolph S. Foster, both
to become members of Drew's first faculty.[67] Despite such open and
important advocacy, many Methodists shared the sentiments about
seminaries voiced by Peter Cartwright earlier:

Perhaps, among the thousands of traveling and local preachers employed and engaged in this glorious work of saving souls, and building up the Methodist Church, there were not fifty men that had anything more than a common English education, and scores of them not that; and not one of them was ever trained in a theological school or Biblical institute, and yet hundreds of them preached the Gospel with more success and had more seals to their ministry than all the sapient, downy D.D.'s in modern times, who, instead of entering the great and wide-spread harvest-field of souls, sickle in hand, are seeking presidencies or professorships in colleges, editorships, or any agencies that have a fat salary, and are trying to create newfangled institutions where good livings can be monopolized, while millions of poor, dying sinners are thronging the way to hell without God, without Gospel; and the Church putting up the piteous wail about the scarcity of preachers.[68]

Phase I: Biblical Institutes

Faced with such suspicion, Boston area Methodists elected to term the first successful venture, a "Biblical Institute" not a seminary. It opened it in 1839–40 at Newbury, Vermont. Moved later to Concord, New Hampshire, and then again to Boston, it became Boston University's School of Theology, opening in 1867. Among its important achievements was launching the career in theological education of its great symbolic personification, John Dempster.[69] Dempster taught theology at Newbury and Concord but also oversaw the fundraising and promotion of the institutions. He played similar roles in founding the second theological institution, Northwestern (later Garrett) Biblical Institute, which opened in 1854 (Northwestern University developing as an adjacent institution and Dempster delivering the inaugural address).[70]

The two biblical institutes offered a curriculum to prepare Methodists for ministry. Neither, however, in their biblical institute phase, presumed or required that students possess a prior college degree. However, Stephen M. Vail, who converted columns from the *Northern Christian Advocate* into a book-length defense of the Biblical Institute at Concord, advised candidates to conclude "their literary and

46

scientific studies" before entering. The "Constitution and By-Laws" put the expectation somewhat more vaguely:

> Applicants for admission to the regular course of study are required to have a thorough knowledge of the common English branches, and also a good knowledge of the higher English, and of the Greek Grammar; the Faculty, however, are allowed to suspend the operation of this rule, if, in their judgment, it may, in any case, be desirable.[71]

Their programs, then, like counterpart Methodist colleges, had to take candidates where they were, undertake remediation if needed, and build sometimes on fairly basic educational foundations.

The explicit case for an Andover-like post-baccalaureate theological education came the same year, in 1853, from James Strong, graduate of Wesleyan University, later to publish his *Exhaustive Concordance of the Bible* and ten volume *Cyclopedia of Biblical, Theological and Ecclesiastical Literature*, but then president of the Flushing Railroad. Writing in the *Christian Advocate and Journal* (the *USA Today* for the nineteenth century), Strong echoed the argument for higher education by then commonplace:

> The demand for superior theological training in our Church shows itself in a two-fold form, arising from the upward tendency of Methodism, like many other successful and progressive principles, from the lower to the higher stratum of society. As our congregations increase in number and wealth, they naturally increase likewise in intelligence, either by a gradual improvement in the mental culture of the mass, or by the introduction among them of persons of more than ordinary learning and refinement. These congregations cannot now be satisfied with the quality of preaching, in a literary point of view, with which they once were.

Failing to keep pace with its own laity, Methodism was already losing members who "presently withdraw to other Churches where they are favoured with preaching more congenial to their minds." Strong made that same point in several different ways, hazarding the judgment that half of those brought through Methodist Sunday schools flee to other denominations "or back again into the world."

A similar assessment, focused on ministers, constituted Strong's second argument for theological education. Preachers with the talent, education, and aspiration to serve such a changing church have to resort to theological schools of other denominations. "Six members out of a single class at the Wesleyan University, within my knowledge, entered theological seminaries that belong to other denominations. . . ." And he thought similar sorry statistics could be cited as evidence for "Dickinson College, and doubtless at all our Methodist colleges."

Apparently not wishing to offend, Strong trod gingerly with respect to the Concord Biblical Institute and the biblical or theological departments added "in nearly all our colleges." For the further, post-college training that candidates want, he said, "We may point them to Concord or elsewhere within our own denomination to attain it; but they feel even these institutions to be inadequate."

Strong was less reserved with respect to the course of study:

> I know it will be said that the course of study required of preachers after joining the conference is intended and sufficient to supply the special theological preparation needed. This is no doubt to a great extent to the object of this prescription; but any one who has the slightest opportunity of observing how hastily these studies are gone through by the candidate, and how superficially he is generally examined upon them, will at once perceive how indifferently this method meets the requirements of the case. Very few who enter upon them are prepared by previous study, for a thorough theological routine; and those who are, find the prescribed course altogether too popular and circumscribed for their advanced position. It is idle to propose the meager outline appended to the *Discipline* as an adequate course of theology for the present day.

Phase II: Meeting the Demand

Calling for a "central theological seminary" in the New York City area, Strong thought it ought "to take students who have regularly graduated at college, and carry them forward through a full course of Biblical and theological study. . . . A thorough academic preparation must be insisted on as condition of admission. All who enter, of course, would have the ministry more or less distinctly in view; but I would not require the students to be absolutely exhorters or preachers, or to be recommended as such by a quarterly conference."[72]

In 1855 Randolph S. Foster, then a New York pastor who would join Strong on the Drew faculty and later be elected bishop, echoed the analysis and prescription:

The Church needs a thoroughly-educated and liberally-informed ministry . . . as including a thorough training to habits of study, and extensive cultivation in the entire circle of the sciences, and of all human knowledge, so far as practicable, bearing directly or remotely on theology.

Perhaps with an eye to critics, Foster insisted on the importance of balance in theological education, "Methodism needs a more spiritual and consecrated ministry."

We want prophets of the closet [prayer], as well as study [for time with God and with God's Word and other books] men whose hearts glow while their intellects shine: who feel deeply, as well as think profoundly: who experience, as well as theorize: consecrated, as well as ordained: men, who walk with God and who are entrusted with his secrets: who go before the Church, and say, "Follow us as we follow Christ."

To those who doubted—"*The thing can never be: a ministry of this kind? a ministry so learned, and yet so consecrated; so intellectual, and yet so spiritual; so much culture, and yet so great zeal.*"—Foster appealed to examples in the history of the church to insist that education need be no foe to religion. Great learning and great devotion, light and heat, wisdom and love can and must go together.

We must have it: culture and zeal, light and heat, mind and heart! Blended, they will give us power with men and power with God, and we shall prevail. Deprived of them, we shall sink down, down, down in weakness and imbecility, until not a historic vestige will be left of a people who might have been great for God in the earth.[73]

49

Theological education on the Strong and Foster agendas became a centerpiece of the highly successful Centenary financial campaign and among its beneficiaries, Boston, Garrett and Drew Theological Seminary, chartered in 1867 but opened the prior year.

The other Methodist-related denominations followed. The United Brethren opened Union Biblical Seminary in Dayton in 1871. The Evangelical Church followed in 1873 with its own Union Biblical Institute (Naperville, Illinois). Vanderbilt, the MECS's flagship university opening in 1875, featured a divinity school. And the Methodist Protestants launched Westminster Theological Seminary in 1884, site of Western Maryland College.

The several schools, of course, had to contend with Cartwright-like attitudes from the start and, especially, the suspicion that such institutions would breed heresy. William F. Warren, the head of Boston University School of Theology, soon to be the long-term president of the university as a whole, addressed such concerns by insisting that the examination of character would be an ongoing check on the orthodoxy of the MEC theological schools (Boston, Garrett, and Drew) and their faculties. Warren assured northern Methodists with regard to seminaries:

1. Each is officially placed under the direct supervision of the bishops of the Methodist Episcopal Church.
2. No professor can be appointed to any chair in any of the three institutions without the concurrence of the bishops.
3. In at least two of them no professor can take his chair until, in the presence of the Board of Trust, he have signed a solemn declaration, to the effect that so long as he occupies the same he will teach nothing inconsistent with the doctrines and discipline of the Methodist Episcopal Church.
4. At the *Annual Conference examination of character*, every professor—save one who chances to be a layman—is each year liable to arrest if even a rumor of heterodoxy is abroad against him.
5. Each institution is inspected, and its pupils annually examined as to what they have been taught, by visitors delegated from adjacent annual conferences.

6. Each has ecclesiastical qualifications affecting the appointment of trustees.
7. Each is required to report to every General Conference.[74]

Seminaries increasingly would play incredibly important roles going forward. For one thing, they brought the church's intellectual leadership together and focused it specifically on matters theological. Also, the churches (especially the MEC) had come to view their various educational institutions as a system, transforming in 1892 its Board of Education into the University Senate and authorizing it to play accrediting roles (initially over colleges).[75]

However, the seminaries trained only a small portion of those entering the itinerancy—colleges and the course of study continued to be the primary shapers of ministry into the twentieth century.[76]

Phase III: Adding Rigor

Recognition of Methodism's continued dependence on colleges and the course of study and an implicit case for more reliance on collegiate training came from Franklin C. Woodward of Wofford College and the MECS. The course of study delivered preparation and a poorly equipped ministry, he thought, which Methodism's increasingly cultured laity could no longer abide and from whose ministries and congregations they well might well flee. The tests, he declared, are made "far too easy." "There is," he insisted, "probably no learned profession to which access is so free."

Woodward complained that a "man may enter the itinerant ranks without giving to preparation for his great work as much time and pains as would be required to make him a good journeyman carpenter!" So the church suffers with ministers who are "ignorant of the world's thought and progress, of science and literature, of Methodist doctrine and polity, of theology and Church history; men who have no love of reading and study, and who do neither—who cannot read understandingly the Book they pretend to teach, who cannot write a correct complex sentence, or understand it when written; men, moreover, who would not be thus burdening the Church and demoralizing its ministry if a moderately fair test had been applied in their admission. . . ."

Unlike Cartwright, Woodward thought "The itinerancy is a fine field for trained laborers, but a bad place for crude apprentices" because "to the man void of literary resources self-education is almost an impossibility. . . ."

> Unfortunately, the call to preach is not understood to be a "call to prepare," but rather as an equivalent for preparation. . . .
> The Methodist ministry is the paradise of ease-loving indolence, the refuge of secular failures. . . .
> It is too much to ask of cultivated men and women to listen patiently Sunday after Sunday, month after month, year after year, to solecism, historical blunders, false exegesis, worn-out arguments, travesties of the gospel, caricatures of truth! . . .
> It would not be demanding too much of applicants for this high calling to insist upon their taking a thorough collegiate course (see **Appendix**).[77]

A remedy, undertaken in the northern church, was to make the course of study into quite an enterprise, comparable really to a theological seminary, indeed to the college-seminary nexus, as that of the Philadelphia Conference illustrates. The 1896 *Discipline* prescribed a separate course for those on trial, for local preachers, and for class leaders. It also featured courses for both traveling and local preachers in German, Norwegian and Danish, Swedish, Italian, and Spanish. By 1920, the *Discipline* prescribed the courses for traveling and local preachers in the various languages and differentiated the courses for the language conferences in the U.S. from those, for instance, for Norway and Sweden. And it had added courses in Finnish, Russian, Bulgarian, and French. A "Note" directed those needing courses "in Ojibway and in the languages of Africa, India, Malaysia, China, Japan and Korea" to see the "Year Books of Annual Conferences and Missions." A separate course "For Deaconesses" followed.[78]

In 1897, adhering to the greater specificity in the *Discipline* (1896) for the "Method of Conducting Conference Examinations,"[79] Philadelphia adopted a rigorous, detailed program recommended by its Board of Examiners, Thomas Neely chair (and later bishop). Neely and company envisioned a real schooling of the candidates and divided the assignments for each of the four years into three examinations—for June, December, and the day before annual conference (a spring meeting). The abbreviated form of this program, as legislation for conference action (see **Appendix**) required candidates to produce a syllabus for each assigned book demonstrating mastery thereof and written sermons and exegetical studies. It permitted either written or oral examinations, "passing" stipulated as 70 and above. Lectures on exam days and a Ministerial Institute augmented the study that candidates would undertake on their own.

In June, the first year class was to be examined on John Miley's *Systematic Theology 1* (pages 1–266), Henry Martyn Harman's *Introduction to the Holy Scriptures* (pages 1–109), Charles Horswell's *Suggestions for the Study of the English New Testament*, a written sermon, and a syllabus on William Arthur's *Tongue of Fire*.

In December that class was responsible for the rest of Miley 1, Harman (pages 110–447), Adam S. Hill's *Principles of Rhetoric*, to undertake exegetical studies in the Gospels, and to produce syllabi on Thomas Neely's *Governing Conference in Methodism* and John Wesley's *Sermons 2*.

At the annual conference examination, the first year had responsibility for George Park Fisher's *Outlines of Universal History*, John Wesley's *Plain Account of Christian Perfection*, J. M. Buckley's *Theory and Practice of Extemporaneous Preaching*, an essay with syllabi of William W. Martin's *Ecclesiastical Architecture* and of Daniel Dorchester's *Problem of Religious Progress*.

Neely's committee provided candidates more detail in a section of the conference minutes entitled, "Conference Examinations," which was designed to explain procedures to candidates. It indicated due dates for written material and listed the examiner for each book or assignment. It gave the candidates the reassurance that "about two hours will be allowed for each subject." The guidance also clarified what qualified a candidate for admission (and what did not). The committee indicated that college or seminary did not substitute for the course and producing a degree or certificate of advanced study did not free one from the burdens so carefully outlined: "The Annual Conference negatived a proposition to take certificates in lieu of examinations. All candidates, therefore, will be required to pursue the course of study, and to pass the examination thereon."[80] (By 1912 the conference must have decided that three exams a year taxed the Board of Examiners as much as the candidates and contented themselves with two examination periods a year.)[81]

Results

Methodism's continued reliance on the course of study and to some extent on college was well demonstrated in the 1920s by studies of ministerial training—not all glowing with praise at their findings. On that note one introduced itself:

> This study grew out of the widely held belief that the machinery and the methods used in educating Protestant ministers were inadequate. It was asserted that the number and the quality of ministerial candidates had been on the decline for some time and that the churches faced a crisis because of the real or the prospective dearth of leaders.[82]

Another study, based upon indications of educational status in the 1926 Federal Census, showed that 24 percent of MEC ministers had both a collegiate and seminary education. Statistics for the southern church were worse. Of its urban pastors 28.6 percent had *neither* a college or seminary degree and 54.4 percent of rural ministers had *neither*.[83]

Yet another study, for the northern church by Margaret Bennett, was based on responses by 11,275 of the MEC's 14,072 effective members and probationers—an 80 percent return. It identified seven educational levels—8th grade or less, high school incomplete, high school complete, college incomplete, theological school without a college degree, college complete, and both seminary and college complete. The latter three populations, Bennett reported, as 1,311, 2,791 and 2,287 respectively or 11.63 percent, 24.75 percent and 20.28 percent. So barely 20 percent had lived into the program that James Strong had advocated. And the statistics declined among the numerous white European language and the African American conferences. Of the former, only 51 of the 441 total had both college and seminary. Of Black pastors,

86 of 1,183 had both degrees, 58 were college graduates, and 252 had the theological but not collegiate formation. Educational levels also dipped among rural and southern ministers.[84]

However, readers might have taken some comfort in trends. Bennett's comparison of educational achievements at five-year intervals (1901, 1906, 1911, 1916, and 1921) showed an upward trajectory, as also breaking out educational level by age cohort, the younger showing greater tendency to receive both degrees.[85]

By the 1920s, the Methodist family of churches had birthed a number of new seminaries with a wide range of results:

- They ranged in size, quality, type, and constituency, as various studies documented.
- They did assemble the church's theological leadership.
- They established templates for ministerial formation.
- They produced studies of church and ministry.
- They provided the books that the course of study, the colleges, and the seminaries required candidates to read.
- But scattered as they were, they required any who would attend from any distance to uproot themselves and move to that locale.
- That relocation and residence of students in and around the seminary often created a living-learning theological community. Preachers-to-be roomed together. They studied together. They ate together. They worshipped together. They discussed and/or stressed over their courses, circuit appointments, teachers, and presiding elders. (In some seminaries and later cohorts of married students lived together and spouses joined in the general grousing).
- However, if a school's population of students increased beyond the capacity of nearby assignments and circuits, then the seminary's reliance on the formative role of student appointments was endangered. How then would the schools face the challenge of fitting all their ministers-to-be into the counseled, collegial, and conferenced stages of the church's formational processes?

As seminary enrollments increased, the schools found themselves saddled with some new formational aspirations and responsibilities.

[66] *Christian Advocate and Journal* (NY), July 18, 1834, 186.

[67] On the beginnings of Methodist theological education, see Conrad Cherry, *Hurrying Toward Zion: Universities, Divinity Schools, and American Protestantism* (Bloomington and Indianapolis: Indiana University Press, 1995), 19–24; Miller, *Piety and Profession: American Theological Education, 1870–1970*, 246–70.

[68] *Autobiography of Peter Cartwright*, 408. Cartwright continued the retrospective tirade and echoed it elsewhere. See 408–10 and 484–87.

[69] Richard Morgan Cameron, *Boston University School of Theology, 1839–1968* (Boston: Boston University School of Theology, 1968), 115; A. W. Cummings, *The Early Schools of Methodism* (New York: Phillips & Hunt; Cincinnati: Cranston & Stowe, 1886), 369–72. See Dempster's *A Discourse on the Ministerial Call* (Concord, 1854) and *Lectures and Addresses*, D. W. Clark, ed. (Cincinnati: Poe & Hitchcock, 1864).

[70] See Frederick A. Norwood, *Dawn to Midday at Garrett* (Evanston, IL: Garrett-Evangelical Theological Seminary, 1978), 7–15; Cummings, *The Early Schools of Methodism*, 375–95; Gerald O. McCulloh, *Ministerial Education in the American Methodist Movement* (Nashville: United Methodist Board of Higher Education and Ministry, 1980), 19–25.

[71] Stephen M. Vail, *Ministerial Education in the Methodist Episcopal Church*, with an Introductory Essay by B. F. Tefft (Boston: J. P. Magee, 1853), 188, 236. In "Remarks" on the "Course of Study," the school put the expectation somewhat more loosely: "It is very desirable that young men, before entering the Institution, should be well acquainted with the common and higher branches of an English education. Also it would facilitate them much, in entering upon our course of study, to have a knowledge of the elements of Greek." 234.

[72] James Strong, "A Central Theological Seminary for Our Church," *Christian Advocate and Journal* 28 (Dec. 22, 1853), 201.

[73] R. S. Foster, *A Treatise on the Need of the M. E. Church with Respect to Her Ministry: Embodied in a Sermon, and Preached by Request before the New-York East Conference, May 22, 1855.* (New York: Carlton & Phillips, 1855), 13, 54, 58–60.

[74] William F. Warren, "Ministerial Education in Our Church," *Methodist Quarterly Review*, 54 (April 1872), 246–67, 260. The italicizing in (4), which is not in the original, should alert Methodists today of how fully the denomination once exercised oversight of seminaries.

[75] See the Report No. II Committee on Education concerning "The Board of Education" in the Appendix. On the University Senate, see Beth Adams Bowser, *Living the Vision: The University Senate of The Methodist Episcopal Church, The Methodist Church, and The United Methodist Church, 1892–1991* (Nashville: Board of Higher Education and Ministry/UMC, 1992).

[76] See Warren, "Ministerial Education in Our Church" on Course of Study and why it no longer performed satisfactorily (Appendix).

[77] Franklin C. Woodward, "Methodism and Ministerial Education," *Southern Methodist Review* (Nov. 1886), 208, 212–214, 216–217.

[78] *Discipline*/MEC 1920: 591–641.

[79] *Discipline*/MEC 1896: 368–86.

[80] *Official Journal and Year Book of the Philadelphia Annual Conference*, 1897: 174–76. The translation of legislation in directives for the candidates, "Conference Examinations," added further detail, 173–80. See Appendix for the guidance that the MEC bishops gave the 1896 General Conference on formation for ministry. JGC/MEC 1896: 50.

[81] *Official Journal and Year Book of the Philadelphia Annual Conference*, 1912: 180–81. Cf. 1913: 164–67.

[82] Robert L. Kelly, *Theological Education in America: A Study of One Hundred Sixty-one Theological Schools in the United States and Canada* (New York: George H. Doran Company, 1924), vii.

[83] C. Luther Fry, *The U.S. Looks at Its Churches* (New York: Institute of Social and Religious Research, 1930), 63, 73.

[84] On trailing patterns among rural and especially southern rural ministers, see Holifield, *God's Ambassadors*, 153–55.

[85] Margaret Bennett, *The Ministry of the Methodist Episcopal Church: Educational Status and Numerical Strength* (Chicago: MEC Commission on Life Service, n.d), 3, 9, 13, 18, 19, 27–28. Cf. Fry, *The U.S. Looks at Its Churches*, 73.

Synthesized

Seminary Formation Compounded Anew

I term this sixth phase, "Synthesized" or "Seminary Synthesized," but I am perhaps a little too cute in reaching for an "S" or "C" sound. Professionalized might be more apt. Or "clergy-fied," meaning "clericalized." Perhaps the reader will have noted that I have been careful up to this point to honor common Methodist parlance and *not* speak of Methodist as "clergy." Preacher, minister, even pastor. Not clergy!

The middle decades of the twentieth century did finally turn Methodists into clergy and their appointments into parishes. Methodism had, as it were, returned to Epworth.

In his superb study of American ministry, Brooks Holifield breaks the middle decades of the twentieth century into two periods: "The Protestant Ministry Examined, 1930–1940" and "Ministry: From Revival to Crisis, 1940–1970."[86] It seems to me, however, that it makes sense to identify 1920–1960 as the focus on Methodism's theological education.

Methodist theological education, in this period, undertook the heroic task of readying itself to train a Methodism that had seemingly "arrived." But theological education faced the challenges and problems, real or perceived, already mentioned, and it found itself trying to put more aspects of formation together.

New Contexts, New Ingredients, New Pressures

"Synthesis" represented an aspiration for this period and a big one, especially because of the new contexts for, new ingredients in, and new pressures on theological education.

Kelly, who surveyed theological schools in North America, classified them as (1) detached (we today would say "freestanding"), (2) affiliated with a college, (3) university-based, and (4) freestanding but developing into a doctoral institution (think Princeton and Union). Kelly listed Drew as headed towards the latter category, but with the creation of Brothers College at Drew, it might fit uneasily in either the second or third; it originally typified the first. By the 1920s the only Methodist school, I think, in that first, fully freestanding category, was the United Brethren's Bonebrake (now United).

A number of Methodist institutions, some no longer extant, fit that second, college-affiliated or college-proximate type: Westminister (now Wesley) with Western Maryland, Kimball with Willamette, Nast with Baldwin-Wallace, Evangelical with North-Western (College), Central Wesleyan with the college of the same name, Gammon with Clark.

University-based theological education, however, represented Methodism's trajectory. Methodism was on course to do most of its ministerial formation in university contexts—the pattern set by Boston, Vanderbilt, Maclay (now Claremont, then part of the University of Southern California), Perkins, Candler, and Duke. Garrett and Iliff, though not formally schools of Northwestern and Denver, were nevertheless effectively on the university campus and working collaboratively.[87] Westminster moved into proximity to American University in the late 1950s and at about the same time Gammon both nestled amidst the Black colleges and universities of Atlanta and also became a key part of the Interdenominational Theological Center.

As Gerald McCulloh indicates, even schools not proximate to universities would eventually work at developing programmatic relations that achieved something comparable.[88]

The agenda?

First, living fully into the promise and possibility of doing formation in a university context![89]

Second, and also important in setting the theological agenda and stressed by McCulloh, were the Methodist churches' decisions to locate their new schools in urban contexts (some allowance being made, perhaps for Durham). That had not been the counsel or the result when the MEC founded Drew in the 1860s. Denominational leaders then wanted proximity to New York but also a bucolic setting for its ministers-to-be. But by the 1920s Methodist seminarians would have access to the urban resources including the great churches of Boston, Chicago, Dallas, Los Angeles, Atlanta, Denver, and later the nation's capital.[90]

Third was the related factor of Methodism's openness to new theological disciplines—religious education, sociology, psychology of religion, ethics, missions, music, and practical theology.

In Kelly's study of theological education in North America, he undertook a fairly careful comparison of Presbyterian, Episcopal, and Methodist programs. He found considerable homogeneity among the six MEC schools he analyzed. "They lay," he affirmed, "comparatively little stress upon the historical aspect of theological education and put much upon the later developments in the field of religious education and social service." He continued:

> The expansion of the field of pastoral theology is conspicuous in the Methodist Episcopal group. Their programs propose to relate the church to the present social order. They provide numerous courses in religious education; psychology of religion; practical survey methods, both for church and community; sociology; social service; city church; rural church; clinical work, etc. Garrett and Boston are particularly strong in these regards. . . . No group of denominational seminaries is making a more strenuous effort to apply thorough scientific methods to the training of preachers who are to become social engineers and religious educators.[91]

Holding All Together

The curricular expansion of the practical and social scientific disciplines reflected and gave space for Methodism's embrace of social Christianity; its continuing investment in missions—urban, national, and international; its ongoing commitment to temperance; its new passion for world peace; and its growing interest in labor issues.

But how was it all to be put together—the new fields with the classic theological disciplines, the more book-based with the practical, content with skills, the service oriented with the revivalistic, the theoretical with the experiential, the academic with the spiritual, the theological with the formational, knowledge with vital piety?

Methodism had presumed

- that itinerancy itself would achieve the syntheses required for ministry—*magically, automatically, without fail*;
- that converted and under Methodist disciplines, the preacher would find the course-of-study reading program a natural fit; and
- that circuit appointments while reading, doing college, or attending seminary would meld the experiential and theoretical.

Ironically, in enriching the curriculum, adding the various fields that examined and engaged the world, importing the social sciences, enlarging the arena of practical theology, situating their schools in university contexts and selecting urban locales, the Methodist seminaries made problematic—indeed impossible—that older self-actualizing, magical, automatic fail-proof integrating or synthesizing of knowledge and vital piety.

And the various causes and issues with which the churches grappled after World War I broadened and deepened the challenges of holding it all together:

- The war and the war's carnage brought Methodist academics and students to new visions of and commitments to peace, to interests in the causes of war, and to the quest for international disarmament.

60

- Labor discord and violence raised issues of the roles of the church and church leaders in the social and economic order.
- Prohibition and its repeal first invigorated Methodism's sense of its importance in the building of a Christian America and then clarified the improbability of that venture.
- The quest for unification among the Methodist denominations brought into sharper focus the matter of race and the question as to whether Methodism would be an inclusive church.
- And the broader ecumenical movement, its life and work and faith and order challenges, and cooperative endeavors in missions and through the Federal Council of Churches, pressed theological education to envision ministry in ever-broader terms.
- The financial collapse and depression challenged the church in a host of ways, not least of which was the dramatic drop in giving.

Additionally, religious fundamentalism was on the rise, which proved less denomination shattering in Methodism than for Baptists and Presbyterians. But it focused questions about synthesis: Did progressive/social gospel/liberal books and subjects belong on the course of study and in the seminary curricula?

The critics, like Harold Paul Sloan, thought *not!* They wanted the Course of Study, the mandatory, common reading program for all MEC candidates, purged of liberal heresy. They wanted Methodist ministerial formation on the traditional track, believing that itinerancy itself would achieve the syntheses required for ministry—*magically, automatically, without fail!* They seemingly trusted that converted and under Methodist disciplines, the preacher would find the course-of-study reading program a natural fit. And they wanted the older texts so whether reading in circuit appointments, going to college, or attending seminary, the candidates would readily meld the experiential and theoretical.[92] Doubtless, that old format worked for some and in some places.

However, each of the new disciplines within the theological curriculum had its own vision for integrating head and heart, the academic and the practical, theology and ministerial skills, knowledge and piety.

So how was ministerial formation to be put back together, its parts to be reintegrated? Were there models upon which the men who led the church and academy might have drawn?

Overlooked Model: Deaconesses

The integrative challenges recognized in the 1920s had been faced and addressed three decades earlier with curricular and pedagogical initiatives by the visionaries of the deaconess movement and founders of deaconess training schools. Those accomplishments and models, if they helped reshape theological education in the twentieth century, do not seem to have earned very clear footnotes, at least acknowledgments onto which I have stumbled. At any rate, in 1885, Lucy Rider Meyer laid out her vision before Chicago Methodists on "The Training of Christian Workers," calling for a women's order and a training school to prepare them for religious leadership.[93] Two years later and largely through her own fundraising, she launched the Chicago Training School for City, Home, and Foreign Missions (CTS). Still later she opened its living-learning counterpart, the Chicago Deaconess Home.[94]

The 1888 General Conference recognized the office of deaconess and the plan for its work in the United States and abroad. The women of the MEC and especially the Woman's Foreign and Woman's Home Missionary Societies provided financial support. Meyer's husband, YMCA secretary for Chicago, served as the business agent for the school; she, its principal. *The Message*, later the *Deaconess Advocate*, interpreted the school, order, and ministries.

Annual conferences, through a nine-member Board of Deaconesses (three of the nine to be women), oversaw deaconess formation and credentialing. They licensed qualified candidates twenty-five years of age or older who had served a probationary period of at least two years and were recommended by a quarterly conference. In simple long black dresses with bonnets with white ties at the neck, deaconesses were costumed for economy; for "sisterly" community; and for instant recognition, accessibility, and protection as they worked in dangerous urban neighborhoods and among the poor. Unsalaried and single, deaconesses received board, uniform, and a monthly allowance.[95]

Rider Meyer, who regularly taught courses on the Bible, was soon joined by Isabella Thoburn, principal of Lucknow Woman's College in India, then home on leave, and additional faculty from Chicago area ministers, teachers, and physicians. She envisioned a curriculum at once comprehensive, practical, experiential, socially relevant, and ministry-oriented. It included, of course, Bible classes, but also studies in "hygiene, in citizenship, in social and family relationships, in everything that could help or hinder in the establishment of the Kingdom of Heaven on earth." Methodists from rural areas or small towns lived and learned together. And they studied and worked together, fieldwork in the city (including house-to-house visitation among the immigrant poor or in hospitals that served the needy) informing and being informed by the classroom.

All deaconesses in training took the courses in Bible, the *Discipline* of the MEC, historical and doctrinal studies, and methods of social service.[96] Thereafter the training program was geared to the two main types of deaconess ministries—nurse deaconesses and missionary deaconesses (also referred to as visitors or evangelists).

Nurses received theoretical and practical preparation comparable to that of nursing schools. Rider Meyer completed her own medical training at Woman's Medical College of Northwestern University in 1887 and was listed in the CTS catalog as Lucy Rider Meyer, M.D. However, she left the teaching of nursing at CTS to others. Instead, for faculty she drew on Chicago physicians, among them Dr. Isaac Danforth, an early trustee of the school. Danforth helped establish a medical clinic at CTS to provide hands-on nursing training and free medical care to Chicago's poor. He taught human anatomy and Dr. Eliza H. Root taught hygiene and obstetrics. A successor to the clinic, Wesley Hospital, a six-story facility, opened in 1901.

By 1910, the MEC had consecrated more than a thousand deaconesses and by 1915 had opened some sixty religious training schools. Among the more prominent, in addition to CTS, were the New England Deaconess Home and Training School (Boston), the Lucy Webb Hayes National Training School (Washington, D.C.), the National Training School (Kansas City), the National Training School (San Francisco), and the Training School for Colored Deaconesses (Cincinnati). The United Brethren in Christ began deaconess work in 1897, the Evangelical Association in 1903, the Methodist Protestant Church in 1908, and the Methodist Episcopal Church, South, in 1902. The latter's Scarritt Bible and Training School, established in 1892 in Kansas City, Missouri, relocated to Nashville in 1924.[97] The driving force behind Scarritt (and equally prominent for the cause in the MECS to Rider Meyer in the MEC) was Belle Harris Bennett, her name now added to the Scarritt facility.

MEC deaconesses had from the outset been able to pursue candidacy through courses of study prescribed by annual conference deaconess boards. The 1912 *Discipline* carried a brief program outlined by the General Deaconess Board. In 1920, General Conference prescribed a unified, churchwide "Course of Study for Deaconesses."[98] It carried through the social Christianity impetus that had begun to shape northern Methodism. In contrast to earlier curricula, the new course was weighted in the direction of the social sciences, social ethics, and social work theory and method. It now reads like a "Who's Who" of the social gospel and Methodist liberalism—Harris Franklin Rall, Albert Knudson, Donald Soper, Walter Rauschenbusch, Francis Peabody, and Harry Ward.

Here then, in deaconess training, in this early Methodist social gospel experiment, from its inception through to 1920—in urban areas, with access to Methodism's universities, through the new theological fields—the women demonstrated how the various formative processes ought to be and could be put together. Their programs interlaced the new fields with the classic theological disciplines, the more book-based with the practical, content with skills, the service oriented with the revivalistic, the theoretical with the experiential, the academic with the spiritual, the theological with the formational, knowledge with vital piety. Did the men get it?

Did Methodist men take guidance from their women? If the men who led the seminaries looked to deaconess education for a model of how to integrate the myriad strains of theological education, they have not left very clear footnotes of that indebtedness.

What are more clearly acknowledged are two synthesizing ventures that functioned within the largely male universe of theological education.

By the 1930s two new integrative resources were becoming programmatic standards in theological curricula: field education and clinical pastoral education (CPE). Both would prove important in helping students put it all together. CPE became critically important to many clergy in developing counseling skills and certainly in the emergence of the various specialized care-giving ministries.[99] It did not typically become a required course for Methodists.[100]

Prevailing Model: Field Ed

Field education, on the other hand, was already becoming standard and would soon be a requirement in Methodist theological education.

Kelly, who did the inventory of theological education for the 1920s, detailed curricula with some care but had needed no category for and amassed no data on field education.[101] By contrast, in 1934 William Adams Brown and Mark May, who led the studies that issued in the four volume *The Education of American Ministers*, one of a spate of studies of church and ministry in the 1920s[102] and 1930s, devoted a major section, descriptively entitled, to "The Seminary Laboratory: Field Work."[103]

In an initial overview of "The Seminary Curriculum," Brown and May identified four important changes to have taken place over the past quarter century: "the enlargement in the subject matter," permitting students some election of their courses, accommodations for the various forms of ministry emerging, and "changes in educational theory which extend the seminary's responsibility beyond that which is taught in the classroom and put emphasis on what the student learns by doing." They elaborated on the fourth point:

> We note finally a growing tendency toward a more enlarged conception of the curriculum—a conception which goes beyond the course of study and includes all sorts of cultural and educational experiences which the seminary and the community provide. This tendency is reinforced by the growing emphasis in educational circles upon the educational value of practice as a key to knowledge. We learn by doing; and the older view of the curriculum as a body of knowledge to be mastered for its own sake is attacked in many quarters as inadequate if not positively false.[104]

Later in that chapter Brown and May dealt with two emerging tensions pertinent to—indeed critical for—such learning and for synthesizing knowledge and vital piety: *Professional versus Vocational Training* and *Content and Skill* (see **Appendix**).

The vocational school gives the student specific skills in the details of the task he is to perform; the professional school attempts to give him a broad foundation of principles and skill in thinking out practical problems, with the belief that he will acquire the special practical skills when he gets on the job. . . .

The curricula of most seminaries are obvious compromises between the vocational and the professional view. Even where the vocational view is consciously adopted, many seminaries seem to be limiting themselves to the kinds of practical skill that can be developed in the classroom. A few, to be sure, are making place for laboratory or clinical work in parishes, Sunday schools, etc.

With respect to the second tension on content and skill they offered an observation that remains pertinent:

Stated briefly, it is whether or not the curriculum shall be viewed as a body of subject-matter, done up in course packages to be dealt out to and digested by the students, or is it to be viewed as an orderly series of experiences arranged to achieve definite goals. According to the first view, the seminary is a place where the student gets information; according to the second, it is a place where he has educational experiences, only part of which are derived from books. The issue is not so much in the nature of an antithesis as it is a narrower or broader view of the curriculum. The narrower view regards the curriculum primarily as a course of study, the major experiences being book and classroom contacts with teachers; the broader view regards the curriculum as including all educational experiences of the student.

They insisted that "the broader view is easy to take, but hard to carry out in practice. Most seminaries will tell us they subscribe to the broader view; but their curricula are built on the narrower one." The difficulty, they continued, "is that there are so many truly educational experiences that cannot be catalogued and reduced to courses and credit hours."

Here we come upon the outstanding weakness in American higher education. It is course-minded, and credit-minded. Things that cannot somehow be squeezed into the system of courses and credits do not get in. We proceed on the theory that learning is getting information; and that information is contained in books and lectures, which can be classified into courses and properly labeled. Getting an education is, externally at least, a process of passing courses, and rolling up a score of credits, which at the end of a specified time can be cashed in for a degree.

Fieldwork, they noted, represented one important initiative towards this broader conception of education, and they gave that considerable attention.[105] Brown and May concluded their detailed survey of the various designs for field education with this appraisal:

This review of significant experiments in progress must indicate the vitality of the movement to make supervised field work a fully integrated aspect of theological education. Indeed the evidences of effective field work presented in this chapter and the indications of its rapid extension, might with reason lead to the conclusion that supervised, graded experience as the core around which curriculum courses are formed will soon be considered as essential to an adequate training for the ministry as it is now considered necessary to an adequate training for engineering, for law, and for medicine.[106]

The several phases of making "supervised field work a fully integrated aspect of theological education" occurred in fits and spurts in the several schools. Already in the teens, Boston's catalog affirmed, "In departments where it is possible, as the Homiletical, Sociological, the Pastoral and the department of Religious Pedagogy, the student is trained by actual service under the guidance of experts . . . . The School has . . . a laboratory at its very doors." Supervision through a course called "Practical Service" soon followed, and further enhancements came in the 1920s. Another critical phase in the development of the philosophy and practice of fieldwork occurred in the 1950s.[107] At Garrett, on the other hand, Frederick Norwood treated the late 1950s as yielding the dramatic changes in fieldwork, including the production of a sixty-four page Field Education Manual.[108]

The design for a survey of the then ten Methodist seminaries in the mid-1940s had apparently not included close examination of fieldwork but gestured in its importance and implied that it was not uniformly a requirement. It acknowledged that "The traditional theological curriculum was a purely academic one, 'Student charges' were thought of primarily in terms of the economic necessities of prospective ministers. Only gradually did theological educators come to see that the problem was akin to that of normal training for teachers and clinical training for doctors." The study indicated that "it is clear that no one of the ten schools is satisfied with the present status of its Field Work." Then followed ten suggestions of "what ought to be included in a minimum program."[109]

At whatever pace, field education, during the academic year or over the summer or through internships brought the circuit rider, as it were, into the curriculum. Experiential learning, always a Methodist signature, found its rightful place in catalogs and manuals. Experiential learning certainly gained much from the Progressive movement, especially as given pedagogical and curricular directions by the Methodist George Albert Coe, the whole religious education venture, and its professional association, the Religious Education Association.

The New Norm: Professional Ministry

The larger agenda for which Coe and Brown and May pled, namely professionalizing the ministry, proceeded with the Methodist schools certainly playing their part:

- They increased standards.
- They drew in more students.
- They added vocational tracks geared to professionalizing selective ministries—missions, religious education, campus ministry, and social work.
- They collaborated with counterparts from other denominations in the formation in the 1930s of an agency to oversee and

accredit theological schools, namely the American Association of Theological Schools (AATS).[110]

- They pressed to require a college education for admission.
- They augmented faculty, sought doctorates in faculty for fields routinely conferring such, and so increased the overall size and quality of faculties.
- And they mounted four-year, summer course-of-study schools, with scaled down versions of a theological curriculum.

The seminary-trained minister became the norm. And the new Methodist Church symbolized that by equipping clergy with a manual for Sunday mornings—a book of worship, the first since Wesley's *Sunday Service*.[111]

Conferences passed legislation moving in that direction. The trend was indicated in statistics gathered in the late 1940s for the then Methodist Church:

Of the 4,399 effective ministers, only 58.6 percent had both college and seminary degrees but the percentages increased with each younger cohort.

Only 39.3 percent of the effective 1,286 ministers in the 58–72 age group had graduated from both college and seminary;

In the 43 to 57 age cohort (1,556), 57.1 percent had both; and
Among the 1,557 of those under 42, 76 percent had both degrees.[112]

In addition, Methodist seminaries enrolled most of those heading for Methodist ministry.

The same study counted 1,418 students in Bachelor of Divinity (B.D.) programs (plus another 604 in "studies beyond graduation who probably were looking mainly to career other than the pastorate"). Asbury Seminary and various non-Methodist schools enrolled 676 or one-third of the total:

Asbury	144
Union (NY)	98
Temple	80
Vanderbilt	35
Oberlin	32
Pacific School of Religion	27
Chicago	20
Louisville	19
Howard	13
All others	11 or under.[113]

The seminary-trained minister indeed became the norm, the B.D. (now Master of Divinity [M.Div.]) stipulated as required for elder's orders in the 1956 *Discipline*. So John O. Gross could affirm in 1960:

The past twenty-five years have witnessed the greatest period of growth for our theological schools. The B.D. degree has become the basis for admission to the itinerant ministry. This past year 82 per cent of all persons received into full connection were graduates of theological seminaries. In the past decade enrollments in our seminaries have increased 87 per cent. By 1970 the number of men studying in our theological schools should reach five thousand.

Today the atmosphere in our church is more congenial for theological schools than ever before.[114]

Gross went on to comment on the supportive relation between the seminaries and the church's colleges and junior colleges. He might have noted as well but did not need to state the obvious that Methodism's ministry had been a connectional, communal, and hands-on project:

- Begun with an individual's baptism
- Extended through the cradle rolls; vacation Bible school; years of Sunday school, Methodist Youth Fellowship, church camp
- Focused through summer mission trips, a Methodist college, campus ministry, the school's religion courses
- Reinforced with encouragement all along the way by Sunday school and VBS teachers, MYF leaders, camp counselors, religion faculty

- Claimed in a call to ministry
- Resourced in seminary (or course-of-study) and in the apprenticeship placements in fieldwork or student pastorates; and then
- Recognized in the Board of Ordained Ministry and the ordination process itself.

A "pipeline to ministry" some now call it, looking back. Methodist connectionalism at work might say it better.

Whether we speak of breakage at every joint in the pipeline or of the disconnects in the connection, we need to acknowledge that we have been dealing in a different universe for theological education for several decades.

---

[86] Holifield, *God's Ambassadors*.

[87] Kelly, *Theological Education in America*, 213–14. See individual treatments arranged by state. Norwegian Danish and Swedish theological schools were also in Evanston. See McCulloh, *Ministerial Education in the American Methodist Movement*, 66–70. For reflection on Kelly's study, see Miller, *Piety and Profession: American Theological Education, 1870–1970*, 314–39.

[88] See McCulloh, *Ministerial Education in the American Methodist Movement*, 83–93.

[89] See especially Cherry, *Hurrying Toward Zion: Universities, Divinity Schools, and American Protestantism*.

[90] See Kelly, *Theological Education in America*, 55, for a chart comparing the urban contexts for theological education of major Protestant bodies. With its two new seminaries, the MECS was 100 percent urban, the Presbyterians U.S. were 86 percent, and the Congregationalists, Northern Baptists, and Methodists in the 70 percent range; Miller, *Piety and Profession: American Theological Education, 1870–1970*, 246–70.

[91] Kelly, *Theological Education in America*, 97, 98, 99.

[92] MEA 1: 240–42.

[93] MEA 2: 1889, 1893b, 1902.

[94] Lucy Rider Meyer, *Deaconesses, Biblical, Early Church, European, American, with the Story of How the Work Began in the Chicago Training School, for City, Home, and Foreign Missions, and the Chicago Deaconess Home*, 3rd ed., rev. and enl. (Cincinnati: Cranston & Stowe, 1889); Isabelle Horton, *High Adventure: [The] Life of Lucy Rider Meyer* (New York: Methodist Book Concern, 1928); Mary Agnes Theresa Dougherty, "The Methodist Deaconess, 1885–1918: A Study in Religious Feminism" (Ph.D. dissertation, University of California Davis, 1979). On the history of the deaconess movement in the broader United Methodist tradition, see also her book, *My Calling to Fulfill: Deaconesses in the United Methodist Tradition* (New York: Women's Division, General Board of Global Ministries, UMC, 1997) and article "The Social Gospel According to Phoebe: Methodist Deaconesses in the Metropolis 1885–1918," Russell E. Richey, Kenneth E. Rowe and Jean Miller Schmidt, eds. *Perspectives on American Methodism: Interpretive Essays* (Nashville: Kingswood Books/Abingdon, 1993), 356–70.

[95] Lucy Rider Meyer, "Deaconesses and Their Work," in *Woman in Missions: Papers and Addresses presented at the Woman's Congress of Missions, October 2–4, 1893, in the Hall of Columbus, Chicago* (American Tract Society, 1894), 182–97. See also Catherine M. Prelinger and Rosemary S. Keller, "The Function of Female Bonding: The Restored Diaconessate of the Nineteenth Century," in Hilah F. Thomas, et al., *Women in New Worlds*. (Nashville: Abingdon Press, 1981, 1982), vol. 2:318–37. See also Keller

et al., *Called to Serve: The United Methodist Diaconate* (Nashville: General Board of Higher Education and Ministry, UMC, 1987); Elizabeth M. Lee *As Among the Methodists: Deaconesses Yesterday, Today and Tomorrow* (New York: Woman's Division of Christian Service, Board of Missions, the Methodist Church, 1963); Betty Letzig, "The Deaconess in the United Methodist Church" *A Presentation to the Committee to Study the Ministry of the Council of Bishops,* December 1993; and Letzig, "Deaconesses Past and Future," *New World Outlook* (May–June 1992) 29–31.

[96] Dougherty, "Methodist Deaconess," 46, 147. See also Horton, *High Adventure,* 154–57.

[97] This paragraph is largely taken from MEA 1: 314 and this entire discussion draws on MEA 1: 308-21.

[98] See *Discipline/MEC* 1912, ¶609, 567–68; *Discipline/MEC* 1920, ¶665, 639–41.

[99] See E. Brooks Holifield, *A History of Pastoral Care in America: From Salvation to Self-Realization* (Nashville: Abingdon Press, 1983), chapters 5–8.

[100] Stephen D. W. King, *Trust the Process: A History of Clinical Pastoral Education as Theological Education* (Lanham: University Press of America, 2007); Charles E. Hall, *Head and Heart: The Story of the Clinical Pastoral Education Movement* (N.p.: Journal of Pastoral Care Publications, 1992); Edward E. Thornton, *Professional Education for Ministry: A History of Clinical Pastoral Education* (Nashville and New York: Abingdon Press, 1970); Stephanie Muravchik, *American Protestantism in the Age of Psychology* (Cambridge: Cambridge University Press, 2011).

[101] Kelly, *Theological Education in America,* 68, 70, 72, 75, 78–79, 82, 113–27.

[102] See the important study by the Interchurch World Movement of North America, *World Survey* (New York: Interchurch Press, 1920).

[103] William Adams Brown and Mark May, *The Education of American Ministers,* 4 vols. (New York: Institute of Social and Religious Research, 1934), 3: 192–251. On the Brown/May study, see Miller, *Piety and Profession: American Theological Education, 1870-1970,* 470–89.

[104] Brown and May, *The Education of American Ministers,* 3: 35–36.

[105] Brown and May, *The Education of American Ministers,* 3: 57–59.

[106] Brown and May, *The Education of American Ministers,* 3: 251.

[107] Cameron, *Boston University School of Theology,* 50–51, 124–25.

[108] Norwood, *Dawn to Midday at Garrett,* 187–88.

[109] *A Survey of Ten Theological Schools Affiliated with The Methodist Church under the Auspices of the Commission on Theological Education, the Board of Education and the Association of Methodist Theological Schools* (Nashville: Department of Educational Institutions, n.d.), 385–89. Among the desiderata: putting "the educational objective first," permitting various kinds of placement, getting all remunerative arrangements under school authority, requiring contracts, reports, and supervision, using summers, exploring internships, making fieldwork a requirement, and tailoring placements to maturity and experience.

[110] Holifield, *God's Ambassadors,* 231–32.

[111] *The Book of Worship for Church and Home. With Orders for the Administration of the Sacraments and Other Rites and Ceremonies According to the Use of The Methodist Church* (N.p.: The Methodist Publishing House, 1945).

[112] *A Survey of Ten Theological Schools Affiliated with the Methodist Church under the Auspices of the Commission on Theological Education, the Board of Education and the Association of Methodist Theological Schools* (Nashville: Department of Educational Institutions, n.d.), 28. See Paul N. Garber, *The Methodist Ministry 1959* (Nashville: Department of Ministerial Education, 1959), 39 for a somewhat different overall estimate.

[113] Ibid. 358, 441–43.

[114] *Discipline/MC* 1956, ¶¶ 342, 343, 324; John O. Gross, "The Methodist Church and Theological Education," *The Ministry in the Methodist Heritage,* Gerald O. McCulloh, ed. (Nashville: Department of Ministerial Education, 1960), 129–43, 133. The book contained papers presented at a Convocation of Methodist Theological Faculties, including one of my father's.

Contextualized

Varying Pedagogies and Curricula

On this stage, the reader—if faculty or staff in seminary today—could write perhaps as well as I. Certainly, most now teaching would have been trained and/or given leadership in shaping this seventh style. It reigns today, albeit much battled.

In the 1960s and 1970s, training for ministry turned yet another corner in quest of professional status. The old Bachelor of Divinity became the Master of Divinity, and the Doctorate of Ministry (D. Min.) signaled aspirations on the part of schools and clergy to reclaim the ancient parity with medicine and law. A cluster of important ministries achieved new credential status, first as diaconal ministers and later as deacons.

The contextualized phase might be regarded as beginning in the 1960s, but especially gaining momentum from the 1970s. Perhaps 1968—the formation of United Methodism, the birthing of caucuses, and the creation of the Ministerial Education Fund[115]—would be a date with which to reckon.[116]

Formational Pressures

At any rate, theological education in the latter decades of the twentieth century had much with which to contend. (Among the resources for understanding the plight of and solutions for theological education is the aptly titled, *Theological Education*, the journal of the Association of Theological Schools.)

What forces shaped ministerial formation in this period? Each of these exerted pressure and had influence:

- Civil rights, anti-war, and anti-poverty initiatives of that era and their echo within theological education;
- Fuller integration of historically white seminaries but also white flight that emptied out America's cities, brought urban decay, and doomed so many of the church's downtown "cathedral congregations";
- The growing numbers of women students in seminary, among clergy, and very gradually on faculties; slowly as well the welcoming of feminists onto faculties and of feminism into theological curricula;
- Disparate vocational and learning agendas within the school, especially with students aspiring to quite an array of ministries and/or service careers;
- The explosion on the American social and political scene of conservative-evangelical Protestantism and the slowly dawning awareness by the mainline that their hegemony over American society was over;
- Ecumenical and interreligious agendas birthed by Vatican II and various World Council of Churches' initiatives;
- Diminished denominational consciousness in the broader culture, but patterns of hyper-denominationalism in boards of ordained ministry;
- Second career, dual vocation, older, and denominationally diverse student cohorts;
- Increased non-residential student populations, the waning of the dorm and of the refectory as contexts for formation;
- Students who showed up with "about five days of post-conversion Christian life," with little or no experience in local churches, and with the desperate need of catechesis;
- New (and old) disciplines of spirituality and programs for spiritual formation to help ground students personally and communally;

74

- Complex interplay within schools and in the church of multiple curricular, pedagogical, and formational visions, especially as informed by the various liberation theologies and reform agendas;
- Complex formational and educational schemes designed to train persons as diaconal ministers (and then deacons) and to do so mindful of relevant curricula and degree programs beyond or beside theological seminaries; and
- Pressures from judicatories to ignore all the "noise" and manufacture graduates/candidates who could "fix" all that was ailing in the churches.

Faculties—growing ever more reflective of the theological, denominational, and vocational cacophony—

- tried to cope;
- subjected themselves to sensitivity training;
- went on immersion trips and sought to incorporate global or international experiences in M.Div. programs;
- revised curricula and pedagogies;
- experimented with new models, new locations, new visions of theological education;[117]
- found themselves engaging and engaged by fragmented, sometimes ideologically differentiated, student cohorts;
- taught out of a variety of perspectives, convictions, theologies, and methodologies;
- undertook doctorate-level teaching and brought such platforms back into the masters program;
- experimented with one sort of contextualization or another;
- launched new fields, including congregational studies and leadership education;
- created or recreated vocational tracks in the M.Div. (and added a variety of other masters degrees dedicated to a vast array of specialized ministries);
- added new joint-degree ventures in the health sciences, conflict resolution, ecological studies;
- gradually embraced new delivery systems, media, digital teaching resources, and the World Wide Web.[118]

And schools and their deans attempted to sustain relations with bishops, conferences, and agencies all the while finding the numbers and percentages of United Methodists on faculties dwindling, as also those who attained the M.Div. and were ordained.

Formational Communities

Accentuating the confessional, theological, and vocational diversity and strains within theological faculties were the various methodologies, perspectives, agendas, and prejudices that shaped religious studies in the final decades of the twentieth century, sometimes doing so vis-à-vis theology and theological studies.

Even in the universities with divinity schools and in the seminaries cooperating with universities for doctoral studies, theological and religious studies sometimes lived in quite unhappy marriages. Religion departments there as elsewhere gave up or had long since given up the Old and New Testament courses and Christianity-normed degree requirements that had been staples and that eased the transition from college to seminary, consequently shattering the undergraduate religion curricula that once had so closely resembled seminary programs. The religion department and seminary might unite in a doctoral program, but the union was not always a holy one. Nor did the department feed its baccalaureates, those who did entertain ministry, into the on-campus seminary in significant numbers.

The deteriorating or ignoring or marginalizing of church-relations by our United Methodist universities, as also by our colleges, is a huge topic and beyond what can be treated here. Suffice it to say that local factors, key players in schools and departments, finances, space, and above all the university (or college) presidents had much to do with how seminaries fit into the university ecology.

I spent many years at Drew under two presidents, both of whose fathers were bishop. One just about destroyed the seminary. One worked at rebuilding it and enhancing the university's relation with The United Methodist Church. But even in the latter instance, where there was will to keep college and seminary working together and in some relation to the church, the larger dynamics of higher education militated against the preservation of these key pieces of the old pipeline from cradle-roll to ordination. Important leaders in Drew's college faculty—some seminary trained, some ordained, many devout Christians—nursed no ill will towards United Methodism and certainly were not intent on dividing school from church but nevertheless in following trends in higher education helped chart directions and build programs that simply left the church behind.

That university and many colleges might remain on the University Senate's list and be nominally United Methodist, but they increasingly hired leadership and faculty who were not. And even where presidents, UM or not, strove to better church relations, they found little with which to work either within the university or in the church. Indeed, the UMC in places where I have served, and I suspect in most other contexts, has long since lost the capacity for and perhaps a strong interest in providing any meaningful support for college or university.

The point here, then, is that whether or not central administrations enthusiastically supported or just tolerated the seminary, the dynamics of religious studies and the overall trajectories in higher education tended to marginalize the divinity or theological school.

Some counter trends have occurred where the seminaries work more closely with law, nursing, public health, medicine, business, or other professional schools on shared or comparable pedagogies, vocational issues, or policies.

In this environment, one might speak of formational *communities* in the plural—various contextualizations of theological education, shaping and guiding different cohorts of students.[119] Indeed, within a given theological school, differing faculty intellectual perspectives, student participation or non-participation in chapel, caucus domination of student activities, commuting patterns limiting peer-learning opportunities (and use of the library), and selections made for certain formational experiences (field education, internships, travel seminars) can produce quite different ministers-to-be, seemingly from one institution.

For a fragmented theological community, the challenge of serving a connection, itself fragmented, constituted one of the motivations that led the Association of United Methodist Theological Schools (AUMTS), the Council of Bishops (COB), and GBHEM to develop *A*

Wesleyan Vision for Theological Education and Leadership Formation for the 21st Century.[120] I call attention to this document as worthy, especially since crafting a single "right" statement for this phase has proven difficult, given the sheer diversity in formational processes, agendas, and styles (see **Appendix**). See also the COB's own ruminations (also **Appendix**).

In this increasingly diverse environment, how would the UMC's seminaries collectively or singly prioritize programs within and/or in relation to the diverse formational communities operative within or in relation to seminary? Would diversity or chaos reign? Or would a seminary stamp order on the formational communities? If so, to which of the various community voices would it—should it—give priority? And how should seminaries orient systems within to the order and disorder of the church locally, regionally, nationally, globally? In United Methodism, at least in the United States, theological education and formation for ministry have faced and now face some interesting challenges and opportunities, some relatively new, others fresh versions of older options. Several come to mind. The first two—post-institutional localism and digital connectionalism—we examined initially in the introduction. Let's look further.

Post-institutional "Localism"

The first challenge surfaced most dramatically at the 2012 General Conference in Tampa in the agendas represented in and stimulated by "A Call to Action." Seminaries were not the direct targets of the church's (and society's) anti-institutional mood prominently displayed in the proposed radical downsizing of boards and agencies of the church. However, these providers of ministerial formation had and have more at stake than may be realized.

Seminaries would probably survive the dismantling or radical downsizing of the church's agencies. Some could survive the vouchering of MEF. Few would prosper in an atmosphere of ecclesial tea-party politics. Of course, not new at Tampa were concerns over the denomination's corporate structure—its array of boards and agencies at a connectional level—and over its expectation that those would be replicated at every ecclesial level down to the smallest country church. Indeed criticisms over bureaucratic excess and inertia surfaced not long after the 1968 reorganizations that gave structural expression to The United Methodist Church.

Participant-observers in this organizational remake, my Duke colleagues, Paul A. Mickey and Robert L. Wilson (now deceased), served up a multi-charge bill of indictment in their *What New Creation? The Agony of Church Restructure*[121]: bloated, bureaucratic, elitist, inbred, professionalized, unaccountable, over-centralized, quota-driven, overly reliant on consultants, tribally and pluralistically politicized, uncoordinated, patronage-inclined, and confused over purposes. In their view, church bureaucracy had generated its own doctrinal framework, one "secular, managerial and organizational."[122] This judgment and their litany of the church's bureaucratic woes have been often recited, especially by critics on the ecclesial right.

Against such attacks, "the empire" struck back, guided by what its critics took to be a "citadel of darkness," the General Council on Ministries (GCOM). The agency published in the early 1980s a seventeen-volume series, *Into Our Third Century*.[123] The hundred-plus page monographs seemingly probed every aspect of United Methodist life, in some cases echoing the critics. In a self-criticism that might well have been a 2012 speech at Tampa, R. Sheldon Duecker, in one of the concluding volumes in the series reported the paradox or ambivalence that "leadership is desired but feared." Calling for a remedy—"transforming leadership," he conceded:

> The general agencies of the church cannot and should not fulfil this type of leadership. There is widespread distrust of the agencies by pastors and laity alike. Agencies are considered to be far removed from the local congregation, unwilling to respond to correspondence, addressing themselves to clientele other than the local church, creating problems because of controversial stands on social issues, and conducting unnecessary and overlapping functions. For many United Methodists, the general agencies represent "the other church."[124]

Ironically, the general agency that generated this reflective series came for many to symbolize and epitomize just the problem that Duecker outlined. Over three quadrennia, General Conference charged GCOM to conduct a study of the Connection, the subtext of which was that GCOM rid the church of GCOM itself. Three times GCOM undertook an extensive, expensive system-wide study and produced a plan *(to this observer looking very much like an effort to make the whole denomination a giant GCOM)*. On its "third strike," GCOM found itself called "out," sent to the showers, and replaced (at least in its functions) by the Connectional Table.

Adding irony to irony, at Tampa in 2012 the Connectional Table, along with the Council of Bishops (COB) and consultants, birthed "A Call to Action" *(a proposal that to this observer looked very much like an effort to make the whole denomination into a giant Connectional Table)*. To others, and especially to leaders in the general agencies, both "A Call to Action" and "Plan B" must have looked like "Methodized" versions of Republican Tea Party campaigns against bureaucratic structures.

Digital "Connectionalism"

The second challenge and potential opportunity looks not internally at the connection but externally and raises key questions: How will tablets and smartphones—with their capacity to put theological instruction and entire libraries in the hands and laps of candidates globally and to provide for interaction from any- and everywhere—inform, not just GBHEM's UMC Cyber Campus, but the entire production and distribution of the resources for ministerial formation? And, in particular, what do such changes augur for theological faculties and for the various research, investigative, scholarship, advocacy, and teaching roles they play?

Have we finally reached the stage of which Thomas Boomershine prophesied, namely of being Methodist "print dinosaurs" competing in a mammal digital universe—cold-blooded linear print beasts now finding ourselves in a multi-dimensional, multi-app, warm-blooded electronic world.[125]

Have we come to the end of the line?

- For brick-and-mortar residential and learning institutions for ministerial formation?
- For print and print-based theological education, for theological libraries, for a community of reading and learning?
- For assembled-in-one-place theological faculties and for conversation between and across disciplinary lines?
- For ministerial formation through such specialized educational institutions?
- For research and scholarship mediated through print—books, articles, journals?
- For the residential scholarly enterprise and the advancement of learning within seminaries?

Will schools be needed, will faculties be assembled, and will instruction and formation for ministry remain campus-based in a tablet-and-smartphone world?

What place remains for the highly specialized faculties, semester-long instruction, and brick-and-mortar schools as the local pastor cohort, courses of study, and alternative credentialing programs expand?

Are we back to circuit-rider formation, even as institutions we attempt ministerial formation for global, pluralistic, and diverse communities, creating new digital and programmatic linkages between North American theological institutions and counterparts across the globe? Are the UMC Cyber Campus, comparable seminary-based efforts, digital initiatives mounted by colleges and individual congregations, and blogs and pages by individual United Methodists akin to the most primitive Methodist patterns of in-the-saddle ministerial formation, circuit-rider initiative-taking, and bottom-up Methodist evangelism and mission? Will theological-religious publication catch up with "The New Explosion in Audio Books" and outfit commuters across the globe with ears-full of systematic, historical, ethical, and biblical as well as inspirational texts for twenty-first century car, bus, train, and plane "circuit riding"?[126]

Do tea party agendas, the Cokesbury decision to go to online-retail only, and various cyber-efforts in global theological education symbolize—indeed, make real—our return to the day when every Methodist preacher did formation in the saddle and served constituencies as a colporteur, a peddler of religious books—his or her "saddle bags" a Methodism online, with Methodist resources available any- and everywhere?

What Now in a Post-institutional and Digital Age?

Relocations represented by Claremont and Saint Paul schools of theology (patterns that align perhaps with digital and post-institutional interests) add to both the experience from which to draw and the key questions that demand consideration as to how theological education and formation for ministry will or needs to be reshaped.

Claremont relocated formation for ministry—dramatically, conceptually, and religiously—by integrating Protestant, Jewish, and Muslim theological enterprises into a new theological university. The projected program imagined a variety of patterns of interaction between and among the three religious traditions in research and action, professional education, and doctoral studies. Later withdrawing from this new Claremont Lincoln University, the seminary resolved to continue interfaith and interreligious education by cooperating with freestanding schools from other religious traditions. In either case—whether in integrated or cooperative settings—what will ministry look like when imam, rabbi, and pastor train together? And will this relocation inspire other experiments, for instance, even closer patterns of professional formation between theological schools and other forms of professional education—moving beyond joint degree programs to common faculties and programs?[127]

If Claremont's experiment ventures toward new futures, Saint Paul's reclaims one of the oldest of American patterns of ministerial formation—that of living with, learning from, and understudying skilled clergy—and it does so by relocating the school into the facilities of and in relation to the myriad programs of the Church of the Resurrection. The church and the school have a long history of collaboration. What will it look like going forward, being in the same physical complex and augmenting the school's faculty with the roughly two-dozen professional staff of the church (see **Appendix**)? If the congregational location of this experiment recalls the seventeenth and eighteenth century Schools of the Prophets at Harvard and Yale where the fellowship assembled to worship, pray, and ask God for wisdom, the mega-church size of Resurrection signals that this arrangement too is a glimpse of a new day for theological education.

What now for seminaries when any- and everyone seems poised to launch ministry-credentialing programs? What now for seminaries in a tablet and smartphone on-demand communication? What now for seminaries in a cyber-instruction universe? What now for seminaries amidst a denominational anti-institutional mood? What now for formation for ministry when programs relocate into new (or old) contexts, leading to

- The efforts of UMC colleges to make like seminaries and offer ministerial education as they have Masters of Business Administration (MBAs)?
- The credentialing of leaders of all types by mega-churches?
- Various experiments to do training in context?
- Resurgence and pluralizing of course-of-study programs?
- New locations for theological education?

Do we close the book on the way we have shaped our ministry?

Or do continuing and new efforts to do theological education in other sites and in other fashions return us to earlier stages of and approaches to Methodist ministerial formation? Indeed can we learn from the seven prior programs by which the church has shaped leadership?

---

[115] See McCulloh, *Ministerial Education in the American Methodist Movement*, 117–24.

[116] See Norwood's chapter, "Challenge and Response 1968–1974," *Dawn to Midday at Garrett*, 196–225; Miller, *Piety and Profession: American Theological Education, 1870–1970*, 726–78.

[117] See for instance, The Cornwall Collective, *Your Daughters Shall Prophesy: Feminist Alternatives in Theological Education* (New York: The Pilgrim Press, 1980); Joseph C. Hough, Jr. and Barbara G. Wheeler, eds., *Beyond Clericalism: The Congregation as a Focus for Theological Education* (Atlanta: Scholars Press, 1988); Jackson W. Carroll et al., *Being There: Culture and Formation in Two Theological Schools* (New York and Oxford: Oxford University Press, 1997).

[118] Lance R. Barker and B. Edmon Martin, eds. *Multiple Paths to Ministry: New Models for Theological Education* (Cleveland: The Pilgrim Press, 2004).

[119] See, for instance, Barbara G. Wheeler and Edward Farley, eds., *Shifting Boundaries: Contextual Approaches to the Structure of Theological Education* (Louisville, KY: Westminster/John Knox Press, 1991) and those contextual efforts described and espoused by my colleagues in Theodore Brelsford and P. Alice Rogers, eds., *Contextualizing Theological Education* (Cleveland: The Pilgrim Press, 2008). On the varieties of ministries being formed see the several books by Jackson W. Carroll, including *God's Potters: Pastoral Leadership and the Shaping of Congregations* (Grand Rapids: William B. Eerdmans Publisher, 2006) and Carroll and Carol E. Lytch, eds., *What Is Good Ministry?: Resources to Launch Discussion: A Collection of Portraits and Essays about Good Ministry* (Durham: Pulpit and Pew Research Reports, Duke Divinity School Publisher, 2003).

[120] See the GBHEM website at http://www.gbhem.org/sites/default/files/PUB_WESLEYANVISION-THEOEDUCATION.PDF especially "Current Challenges & Opportunities for Theological Education and Leadership Formation," pp. 9–14.

[121] (Nashville: Abingdon, 1977).

[122] Ibid., 26.

[123] *Into Our Third Century* (Nashville: Abingdon Press, 1980–83), guided by GCOM General Secretary, Norman E. Dewire initially edited by Ezra Earl Jones, finally by Alan K. Waltz. The series began with William E. Ramsden's *The Church in a Changing Society* and Waltz's *Images of the Future* (1980) and concluded with R. Sheldon Duecker's *Tensions in the Connection: Issues Facing United Methodism* and Waltz's *To Proclaim the Faith* (1983).

[124] R. Sheldon Duecker's *Tensions in the Connection: Issues Facing United Methodism* (Nashville: Abingdon Press, 1983), 77, 88.

[125] Thomas E. Boomershine, "Does United Methodism Have a Future in an Electronic Culture?" *Questions for the Twenty-first Century Church*, 79–90. See also the following essay, pp. 105–16, by M. Garlinda Burton, "Why Can't United Methodists Use Media?"

[126] "Can You Hear Me Now? The New Explosion in Audio Books," *The Wall Street Journal* (August 2, 2013), Arena, D1–D2.

[127] See Board of Trustees Announces End of Relationship with Claremont Lincoln University, Monday, April 21, 2014, http://www.cst.edu/news/2014/04/21/board-of-trustees-announces-end-of-relationship-wi/; Frequently Asked Questions for Separation from Claremont Lincoln University, Monday, April 21, 2014, http://www.cst.edu/news/2014/04/21/frequently-asked-questions-for-separation-from-cla/; CST Moves to Bolster Interreligious Ties, Friday, May 30, 2014, http://www.cst.edu/news/2014/05/30/cst-moves-to-bolster-interreligious-ties/.

Counseled Again?

*Wesleyan Imperatives—*Episkopé *and Community*

Given where we are—with the anti-institutional stresses on institutions, the pedagogies unleashed by the digital and cyber world, the communications opened up by the latest high-tech product in hand, and the emergence of new systems for minting and credentialing ministers—the big question is still before us:

Where *should* we be? Where should we *want* to go to be effective in forming persons for ministry in the twenty-first century?

Do we get any guidance from the great constitutional historian, John Tigert? He observed,

> Since 1744 the two constant factors of Methodism, (1) a superintending and appointing power, and (2) a consulting body called the Conference, have been continuously operative.... These two factors are constitutional or elemental in the government of Methodism. The system itself changes as either of these elements changes or is variously combined with the other: the disappearance of either is the destruction of the system. Something better might take its place, but it would be also something different. The peculiar economy of Methodism would cease to exist.[128]

Episkopé and Community

Perhaps we can render Tigert's two principles more generally as a superintending power and a consulting body—and theologically, as *episkopé* and community.

We may also find guidance from our Wesleyan heritage. Our first stage, "Counseled Under Wesley's Imperatives," featured four facets:

1. Living into Wesley's counsel as set forth in the "Large Minutes" and in its later form as the *Discipline*—counsel mediated in and by books
2. Learning ministry by doing it
3. Being birthed into ministry and nurtured by the community on a circuit, by the saints on successive circuits, by Methodism as a connectional system
4 Growing spiritually in one's gifts, grace, and fruit

For the moment let's consider the first two of these facets as exercises in superintending (*episkopé*) and the latter two as consultative actions (community). The first two guided formation by precept and example. The second two provided the community within and through which persons lived into that guidance.

Then we might return to the historical stages to ask who or what guided formation, fulfilling the *episkopé* function. Recall the stages:

Counseled	under Wesley's Imperatives and through books
Collegial	by yokefellowed tutelage
Conferenced	in course-of-study guidance and accountability
Collegiate	for Randolph-Macon, Wesleyan, Emory... formation
Seminary	in training at Boston University, Garrett, Drew...
Synthesized	through courses plus CPE and Field Ed
Contextualized	in pedagogies and curricula shaped by various contexts
Counseled again?	in Wesleyan imperatives—online?

So, in succession, the superintending guides from each stage were

1. Wesley through his exhortations and guidance in the "Large Minutes" and *Discipline* (but with considerable responsibility by the individual preacher-to-be).
2. Then the colleague, the senior preacher on the circuit, the yokefellow.
3. Next the conferences through the Course of Study, the guidance on the reading from the bishops.
4. Then the Methodist faculty on the colleges scattered across the land.
5. Next the president and faculty of the few seminaries, including those of other denominations.
6. Then the field educators and/or faculty participating in synthesizing classroom and field experience.
7. And lately the various seminary faculty in the several schools whose contextualizing agenda or ideology or vision or pedagogy best suited specific student cohorts.

Responsibility for oversight, at least in the final formative stages, came, it seems, to be delegated further and further away from where ministry was/is exercised. Even though each of the later stages retained much of the apparatus of the prior stage or stages, nevertheless the critical finishing seemed to be owned by the last.

So, the succession of stages document a series of handoffs, of transitions up the educational ladder, and what now look, in retrospect, like disjointed shifts. And in each phase, those involved in discernment, supervision, and judgment look backward and forward assuming some other phase will or should or has made the decisive call about readiness for ministry.

To be sure, in recent years with the discernment procedures before seminary and the probationary processes afterwards, the church has made some effort to move critical phases of formation away from theological schools. However, these endeavors seem to represent more a "corrective" to the seminary's exclusive playing of the formational role and not an effort to knit the several stages of the formation process together again. Conference activities in the probationary period, for instance, initially conceived by the proposers of this legislation as being undertaken hand-in-glove with the seminaries now seem to be geared to correct or remedy or fix what seminaries failed to do. Allowing certainly for exceptions—and there may be many—there seem to be few strategies for tying local church, district, conference, college, and seminary into a coherent system for ministerial formation.

Yet, surely the church never meant for the stages into ministry to be broken apart. And probably before the mid-twentieth century in the long pilgrimage from the cradle roll through church college to district committee to seminary to board of ordained ministry to ordination, the candidate felt cradled, coached, supported, and watched over by each and all actors on the church's behalf. "Pipeline" puts that gracious pilgrimage crudely—the pilgrimage was the way of salvation. But the metaphor of "pipeline" works well to permit the acknowledgment that there are breaks at every joint.

We can also ask each of the historical stages who or what seemed to be the community in, through, by, or around which persons were formed for ministry and grew spiritually. Who or what constituted the consulting body, the community?

1. Initially preachers were birthed into ministry and nurtured by the community on a circuit, by the saints on successive circuits (including often the "mothers-in-Israel"), by Methodism as a connectional system (see **Appendix**);
2. Then by the presiding elder, the colleague "yokefellow" on the circuit, and the local preachers, exhorters, class leaders, and stewards on a district who gathered for quarterly and camp meetings;
3. Next by the "fathers" and "brothers" who made up one's conference and shepherded preachers through the course;
4. Then by the ministry-bound fellow students and the Methodist faculty at the church's many colleges;
5. Next by the seminary communities—although communities whose student members would be scattered after graduation into multiple conferences;

6. Then perhaps by students who shared proximate field placements or were grouped for discernment or joined in bull sessions or otherwise found one another;
7. And finally in caucus or cause or context or vocational track or carpool through which clergy-to-be negotiated the late twentieth century ideological and programmatic cacophony.

What an interesting array of quite different communities for forming ministry! Ideally a plus sign (+) might connect each successive stage with the prior, perhaps the last excepted.

The Formational Community as "Church"?

Is it appropriate to think of the formational community as, in some sense, "church"?

I realize that some would answer a loud *no* to that query. Indeed, I recall several heated debates with a particular colleague at Drew, a Presbyterian, who argued that the seminary was not a church. The debate had been triggered, perhaps by me, by suggesting that faculty had some obligation to come regularly to chapel.

A question for those teaching in United Methodist seminaries: Is it your experience that United Methodist faculty and perhaps a colleague in preaching or worship attend chapel and other colleagues find better things to do? That has been my experience and observation at several United Methodist seminaries. The question about who attends chapel does not seem to me to be trivial. The faculty who do attend, I believe, view themselves as key players in the formational process and understand the seminary community and its rhythms, including worship, to be essential to that progression. To participate in chapel and kindred seminary events is to affirm that the community forms persons and to accept one's part in that drama.

The question about chapel attendance pertains to the issue at hand: formational community as church. I am willing to hazard the claim of formational community as church because of years of insisting in my writing that the Reformation and Methodist threefold criterion for church—where the Word is preached, sacraments celebrated, and order sought or discipline exercised—was achieved in early Methodism in the quarterly meeting.

A side note: With the 2012 *Discipline* the overall offices of ministry include service, compassion, and justice as well as the classic three (Word, sacrament, and order). Given the traditional relating of the offices of Word, sacrament, and order to the redemptive roles of Christ as prophet, priest, and king, there does not seem to be any concern about these additions lacking a comparable theological grounding. Nor when "service" was earlier added to the classic three offices was there apparently any effort to rethink the offices of Christ in a fourfold fashion or to relate "service" to the three classic rubrics. (For elaboration of this concern see the "Resource Paper" produced for the UMC Committee on Faith and Order.)

At any rate, the quarterly conference in early Methodism required and featured at least the three traditional ministerial roles—Word, sacrament, and order/discipline. So in the quarterly conference, Methodism was most fully "church." The Wesleyan class, lacking sacraments and sometimes the preached Word, did not satisfy the three criteria. Nor initially did the Wesleyan society, a counterpart to today's local church. Only the quarterly meeting or conference by plan and practice exercised all three ecclesial functions (and perhaps the new three as well). In being "church" Methodism did not coop itself up in little buildings. Church happened.

In what sense then has the formational community been church?

In both the first and second formational stages (Counseled Under Wesley and Collegial), the quarterly conference brought together all the formational players. And it was, church.

Annual conferences, in their own way, did, even though restricted to the preachers. There, too, the Word was heard, the sacrament (Eucharist) celebrated, order sought (and service made ready).

So also Methodist colleges. Recall that the Wesleyan University licensed the student as a local preacher through a quarterly conference. That was university-as-church.

Similarly Methodist seminaries offer, or at least did offer, what churches do—Word, order, sacrament. And especially as they through field education reconnected practice and precept, seminaries connected Word, sacrament, and order in their weekly rhythms with those offices in congregations on weekends.

To be sure, the fragmenting of the formational communities in the late twentieth century has certainly tested the seminary's capacity to hold all the competing elements together. And many in theological education would have to admit that increasing numbers of students evade the ecclesial aspect of the seminary experience. They commute in, go to class, ignore chapel and bull sessions, leave for job or home as soon as the day's instructions conclude, and take what little reading they will do home.

So formational community as church? as Methodist connectionalism in miniature? as communion of the saints? as the body of Christ? as foretaste of the kingdom of God? How do we do it now? How can formation as church be configured, how mounted, how insured, in a digital world?

Exercise of *Episkopé* an Infringement?

Have seminaries involved in forming persons for ministry infringed upon, crowded, or usurped the authority of those charged to exercise the teaching office—constitutionally assigned to General Conference, traditionally expected from bishops, and shared in various ways by agencies, elders, deacons, and indeed the whole community?

Again we are talking, at least in some sense and to some extent, about the exercise of the teaching office, of *episkopé*, of superintendency that seminaries now play. Do and did the guidance or the guiders play this key ecclesial role appropriately, legitimately, even deferentially? As my schema charts successive stages of the exercise of the teaching office, of *episkopé*, of superintendency, does it raise problems about who played or is playing that role?

What does it mean for the seminaries and their faculties, for instance, fragmented in so many different ways and credentialed quite diversely to be playing the decisive guiding roles now? To illustrate, in a given school, students taking systematics with one professor might read extensively in liberation areas. Another professor might work off classic texts. Yet another might engage ecumenical or environmental or global or Barthian perspectives. What do we make practically, theologically, and organizationally that different cohorts of students in a single school and certainly in the many schools that train United Methodists receive their critical mentoring from individuals or small groups of faculty with whom they align themselves? What does

91

it mean that candidates for ministry in a conference bring potentially very diverse theological perspectives to their interviews (and sometimes are questioned by clergy and laity theologically way out of date)?

Further, given that the formational authority partakes in some way in the teaching office, of *episkopé*, of superintendency, are we comfortable with the series of handoffs and delegations? Do we not need to work harder at connecting the stages in today's credentialing of clergy, stages that do reconfigure the historic stages—Christian formation in local church, at camp, or on mission trip; pastoral counsel; oversight by the district; college; seminary; board of ordained ministry; and conference?

Really Rethinking Church

What might it mean theologically and ecclesiologically, then, to talk about both formational community and *episkopé*? What does it mean for our doctrine of the church to recognize within today's seminary an ecclesial dimension in its role as a formational community as well as in its exercise of *episkopé*?

Do we need more elastic definitions of "church" and of its faithfulness, mission, and nature? Should the *Discipline*, for instance, rework its statements of the church's mission so as to recognize loci of disciple-making beyond the local church, indeed as diverse and plural?

Do we embrace the community or communities formational for ministry in some way in a Methodist ecclesiology? Does a Wesleyan self-understanding, in holding together formational community and *episkopé* need to attend to both the many communities that function like church and the many exercises of teaching or *episkopé*?

More to the point, does the *Discipline* give us guidance now as we turn to wonder about where we are in theological education? If seminary is church and exercises *episkopé*, how should it configure its life, its field or contextual education, its requirements, its expectations of its faculty?

---

[128] Tigert, *Constitutional History*, 15.

The Way Ahead
Formation for Ministry in a Digital World

What practical implications about formation for ministry in a digital world flow from these understandings of *episkopé* and community? Has the schema of successive stages given us some clues about ordering formational processes given the environment in which we now find ourselves?

If we expand the first of Wesley's Imperatives beyond simply being mediated through print and tap into the wisdom of the subsequent two hundred-plus years of faithfulness of the church, the Imperatives still have relevance and authoritative guidance for answering the question of how to function faithfully in the digital age:

1. Living into the church's *Discipline*-mandated Wesleyan counsel
2. Learning ministry by doing it
3. Being birthed and nurtured by community
4. Growing spiritually in one's gifts, grace, and fruit

All belong to the teaching office. All remain essential in formation for United Methodist ministry—however that comes to be rendered and undertaken.

The first stage provides, as well, some guidance especially needed for a digital or media world, namely that streaming instruction and guiding reading that do not move candidates out of their local set-ting, do not expose them to different contexts, do not expose them to counsel from and experience in different congregations or ministry settings does not replicate the movement from circuit to circuit and of changing mentors as a key to formation. Without that personal and communal guidance and exposure, such efforts of formation fail, fail, fail!

So today, with various digital dimensions to on-campus learn-ing and online alternatives to traditional residential programs, how should ministerial formation achieve something comparable to "Being birthed into ministry and nurtured by the community on a circuit, by the saints on successive circuits, by Methodism as a con-nectional system"?

Similarly, the communal aspects of each of the successive stages need to find some counterpart in theological education for a digital world. The same needs to be said for the teaching office aspects of the successive stages:

The modeling, mentoring, and supervising of the yokefellow scheme, as replicated or reconceived in field or contextual educa-tion, remain vital. And here too, candidates should ideally work with more than one yokefellow and certainly not simply the clergy from his or her own home church.

Conferences do, by and large, stay in touch with their candidates and some have their own detailed version of a course-of-study-like template. However, United Methodism as a whole has lost what the common Course of Study presumed and fostered, namely the real-ity and ecclesial affirmation that individuals were being trained for a common, connectional ministry and would be ordained into one ministry for the whole church. We are unlikely to once again have one set of texts for everyone going into ministry. But how then do instruction, mentoring, and supervising at some level respect what ought to be shared across theological formation? (Again see *A Wes-leyan Vision for Theological Education and Leadership Formation for the 21st Century.*)[129]

The collegiate stage reminds us that the theological enterprise needs to stay engaged with the worlds of knowledge and of education as a whole and that candidates should bring a breadth and wealth of wisdom and experience into ministry. The challenge for seminaries or for new digital enterprises of theological education is *how* to stay engaged when students come from many schools, programs, and majors. Gone are the days when a region's church colleges functioned like farm teams and a seminary could relate to four or five and effectively establish an interactive network.

The seminaries, especially as they added field education, CPE, and more lately spiritual formation, did and do offer the church a rounded pattern of formation for ministry. However, as noted, seminaries need to recognize their place within and honor the multiple formational stages, still very much ongoing. Such acknowledgments must shape their programming, self-understanding, relations with the university (if so situated), and promotional efforts. And seminary leadership may well have to struggle to keep the partnerships in view as digital resources might again tempt schools to imagine their global outreach as self-contained ministerial formation.

And post-institutional localism? Need seminaries concerned with global programming despise or despair of post-institutional localism? As earlier indicated, the schools need to vouch for the importance of the systems that support theological education and indeed the outreach ministries of the church. But as teaching institutions, the seminaries can and should help United Methodists understand that localism and connectionalism go together. Holding the two in creative tension was and must be the Wesleyan way.

The cacophony of the late twentieth century, for all of the challenges that it has posed, should remind all who care about formation for ministry that clergy need to be prepared to live and minister faithfully in an ideologically and religiously diverse world. The task of theological education is huge, including indeed an exercise of *episkopé*, and requires helping the church find ways to reclaim some unity for Christ's body amid the pluralisms. The latter challenge, it seems to me, we have yet to successfully address.

Formation for ministry in a digital world, then, should not take us back to a 21st century version of that first stage as though book or its digital equivalent alone will suffice. We cannot simply leave the individual, mired in his or her particular community, isolated before the computer, permitting him or her to think of church as only that local church to which he or she belongs. United Methodism is bigger and better, more pluralistic, more diverse, and more dynamic than any one local church. Nor should the seminaries behave as though their exciting new digital modes of communication isolate them and their processes from the several formational strands and local settings by which Methodism has equipped its leaders. Connectionalism and localism go together.

United Methodists should be encouraged in today's explorations by the fact that Methodists have refashioned their ministerial programming again and again and again. In the past, Methodism undertook each successive stage to deal with inadequacies in the one or ones prior. What then is the future for formation for ministry? Answers lie in the Wesley Imperatives: living into the church's Wesleyan counsel; learning ministry by doing it; being birthed and nurtured by community; and growing spiritually in one's gifts, grace, and fruit. These Wesleyan Imperatives (all four), especially with their implications for *episkopé* and community, plus the historical perspective of more than two hundred years as seen in the stages, provide a healthy platform on which to build the future of formation for ministry in The United Methodist Church.

---

[129] http://www.gbhem.org/sites/default/files/PUB_WESLEYANVISIONTHEOEDUCATION.PDF See especially "Current Challenges & Opportunities for Theological Education and Leadership Formation" and "Agenda Items in Theological Education and Leadership Formation," 9–17. Accessed 3/20/2013.

Appendix

Stage 1: Counseled

METHODIST PUBLISHING:

The following Books are published by JOHN DICKINS, N 182, Race Street, near Sixth Street, Philadelphia; for the use of the Methodist Societies in the United States of America; and the profits thereof applied for the general benefit of the said Societies. Sold by the publisher, and the Ministers and Preachers in the several Circuits.

The Arminian Magazine, Vol, 1st and 2d at 12L, [Shillings] per volume.

The Rev. Mr. Wesley's Notes on the New Testament in 3 vols. Well bound 17 L.

The same lettered 18 L 6d [pence].

Thomas a Kempis, bound 2 L.

Primitive Physic, bound 3 L.

The Form of Discipline for the Methodist Church, with Treatises on Predestination, Perseverance, Christian Perfection, Baptism, &c. All bound together 3, 6d.

The Experiences of about twenty British Methodist Preachers, well bound and lettered 5L ,7d 1–2.

The Experience and Travels of Mr. Freeborn Garrettson, well bound 3 L.

A Pocket Hymn-Book, containing three hundred Hymns well bound and lettered 3L 9d.

The Excellent works of the Rev. Mr. John Fletcher, published one volume at a time; the whole will contain about six volumes: the 1st and 2d vols. Now published, well bound and lettered at 5 L 7d 1–2 per volume.

An Extract on Infant Baptism, stitched 9d.

Children's Instructions, stitched 6d.

An Abridgment of Mrs. Rowe's Devout Thoughts, bound 1L 10d 1–2.

A Funeral Discourse on the death of that great Divine, the Rev. John Wesley, stitched 1.1d.

The Saints Everlasting Rest will be republished some time in Decem. 1791; well bound 5 L 7d 1–2.

Minutes of the Methodist Conferences, 4d.

As the profits of these books are for the general benefit of the Methodist Societies, it is humbly recommended to the Members of the said Societies, that they will purchase no books which we publish, of any other person than the aforesaid JOHN DICKINS, or the Methodist Ministers and Preachers in the several Circuits, or such persons as sell them by their consent.

Dickins' Booklist 1791.

THE 1789 AND 1790 MEETINGS OF THE COUNCIL:

[The **1789 Council** identified the following as its "Constitution":]

The aforesaid Council, when assembled at the Time and Place appointed by the Bishops, shall have Power to mature and resolve on all Things relative to the Spiritual and Temporal Interests of the Church, viz.

1. To render the Time and Form of Public Worship, as similar as possible through all their Congregations.

2. To preserve the general Union of the Ministers, Preachers and People in the Methodist Doctrine and Discipline.

3. To direct and manage all the Printings which may be done, from Time to Time, for the Use and Benefit of the Methodist Church in *America*.

4. To conduct the Plan of Education and manage all Matters which may, from Time to Time, pertain to any College or Houses built, or about to be built, as the Property of the Methodist Connexion.

5. To remove, or receive, and appoint the Salary of any Tutors, from Time to Time, employed in any Seminary of Learning belonging to the said Connexion.

6. In the Intervals of the Council, the Bishop shall have Power to act in all contingent Occurrences relative to the Printing Business, or the Education and Economy of the College.

7. Nine Members, and no less, shall be competent to form a Council which may proceed to Business.

8. No Resolution shall be formed in such a Council, without the Consent of the Bishop and Two-Thirds of the Members present.

[The **1790 Council** took up publishing as its first order of business:]

Quest. What power do this Council consider themselves *invested* with by their electors?

Ans. First, They *unanimously* consider themselves invested with *full* power to act *decisively* in all temporal matters: And, secondly, that of *recommending* to the several Conferences any new Canons, or alterations to be made in any old ones.

Quest. What can be done to promote the book-business?

Ans. 1, In every District where it is practicable, let some trusty diligent Preacher be appointed, as travelling *book-steward*, to preach, and supply the people with books. 2, In districts where this is not practicable, let every *Member* of the Council diligently recommend to the travelling Preachers, to exert themselves in promoting the sale of books. 3, Let every Member of the Council do what he can to forward his own books, or the books of other Preachers, to the Circuits for which they are designed. 4, Let every Member of the Council do what he can to collect and forward book-money, at least once in every three months, if any conveyance can be found, to *John Dickins,* Superintendant of the book-business.

Quest. Who are appointed as travelling book-stewards, by the order of the Council?

Ans. Philip Cox and *William Thomas.*

Quest. How shall such stewards be appointed for the future?

Ans. Any Preacher, being recommended by the presiding Elder and Conference of a district, as a proper person to act in such business, shall be appointed by the Council, when sitting; and, in the intervals of the Council, by the Bishops.

Quest. What can be done to procur religious experiences and letters for the *Arminian Magazine?*

Ans. Let those Members of the Council who choose it, write a *brief account* of their own experiences; and let all the Members procur such experiences and letters of other persons as appear to be unexceptionable, and send the whole to *John Dickins,* who shall submit it to the inspection of a Committee; and they shall have full power to *publish,* or *suppress,* as may be thought most proper.

Quest. Who shall form such a Committee?

Ans. Richard Whatcoat, Henry Willis, Thomas Haskins, and *John Dickins,* or any two of them.

Quest. What books shall be published in the course of the two following years?

Ans. The Arminian Magazine; the Rev. Mr. Fletcher's *Works; Hymn Books;* the *Saint's Rest;* the *Christian Pattern;* the *Primitive Physic;* the *Form of Discipline; Instructions for Children;* and the *Pamphlet on Baptism.* But the Bishops shall have a discretionary power of preparing the controversy for the Magazine, and publishing such tracts as *they* may think necessary for the benefit of the connexion: And *John Dickins* shall have a discretionary power of limiting the publications, according to the state of finances.

Quest. Shall we publish Mr. Wesley's 4 Volumes of Sermons, before the sitting of the next Council?

Ans. If our finances will admit of it, and a sufficient number of subscribers can be obtained.[130]

BISHOPS THOMAS COKE AND FRANCIS ASBURY ANNOTATE THE DISCIPLINE (1798):

[The bishops on reading, publishing, and selling books:]

Next to the preaching of the gospel, the spreading of religious knowledge by the press, is of the greatest moment to the people. The soul, whilst united to the body, must be daily fed with pious ideas, otherwise it will lose ground in the divine life. Though the Lord is wonderfully kind to those of his children who are so unfortunate as not to be able to read, yet we are to use all the means in our power. And though the bible be infinitely preferable to all other books, yet we are, even on that very account, to study the writings of those spiritual and great divines, who have by their comments, essays, sermons, or other labours, explained the bible: otherwise, we ought not to attend to the preaching of the gospel; for what is *that* but an explanation and application of the great truths contained in the bible. He, therefore, who has the charge of the circuit, is to be diligent in the sale of those books, which according to the judgment of our conferences and bishops, are deemed profitable for the souls of our people.

[Rationale for presiding elders and episcopal appointment thereof:]

2. Another advantage of this office arises from the necessity of changing preachers from circuit to circuit in the intervals of the yearly conferences. Many of the preachers are young in years and gifts; and this must always be the case, more or less, or a fresh supply of travelling preachers in proportion to the necessities of the work could not be procured. These young men, in general, are exceedingly zealous. Their grand *forte* is to awaken souls; and in this view they are highly necessary for the spreading of the gospel. But for some time their gifts cannot be expected to be *various*; and, therefore, half a year at a time, or sometimes even a quarter, may be sufficient for them labour in one circuit: to change them, therefore, from circuit to circuit, in the intervals of the yearly conference, is highly necessary in many instances.

[The traveling deacon:]

This office serves as an excellent probation for that of an elder. No preacher can be eligible to the office of an elder, till he has exercised the office of a deacon for two years, except in the case of missions. For we would wish to shew the utmost attention to the order of elders, and to have the fullest proof of the abilities, grace, and usefulness of those, who shall be, from time to time, proposed for so important an office as that of a presbyter in the church of God. And we judge, that the man who has proved himself a worthy member of our society, and an useful class-leader, exhorter, and local preacher, who has been approved of for two years as a travelling preacher on trial, and has faithfully served in the office of a traveling deacon for at least two years more, has offered such proofs of fidelity and piety, as must satisfy every reasonable mind.

[The Method of Receiving Preachers:]

The due examination of candidates for the ministry is of the utmost importance. The questions proposed for this purpose, in the present section, may be drawn out and enlarged upon by the bishops, as they judge necessary; and, if duly considered will be found to contain in them the whole of Christian and ministerial experience and practice. In respect to doctrines, experience, and practice, the preachers will have passed already through various examinations, before they are received into the travelling connection. Let us take a view of the whole, remembering that our societies form our grand nurseries or universities for ministers of the gospel.

1. On application for admission into the society, they must be duly recommended to the preacher who has the oversight of the circuit, by one in whom he can place sufficient confidence, or must have met three or four times in a class, and must be truly awakened to a sense of their fallen condition. Then the preacher who has the oversight of the circuit, gives them notes of admission, and they remain on trial for six months. 2. When the six months are expired, they receive tickets, if recommended by their leader, and become full members of the society. And to prevent any future complaint on the ground of ignorance, the rules of the society must be read to them the first time they meet in class. 3. Out of these are chose, from time to time, *the leaders of classes,* who should not only be deeply experienced in divine things, but have the gift of preaching, so as to feed the flock of Christ under their care, in due season. 4. Out of these when they discover in public prayer-meetings an extraordinary gift of prayer and some gift for exhortation, are chosen *the exhorters.* 5. Out of the exhorters, who are employed in the places of least consequence, or to fill up the place of a preacher, in cases of necessity, are chosen *the local preachers.* These are first to receive a license signed by the presiding elder, and by the quarterly meeting, which is composed of the local preachers, stewards, and leaders of the circuit. Without the consent of the presiding elder, and of the majority of this meeting, which is the most proper and respectable representation of the circuit that perhaps can possibly be devised, no one can be admitted as a local preacher. And the license above-mentioned must be annually renewed, till the local preacher be admitted into the deacon's office. 6. Out of the local preachers are chosen *the travelling preachers,* of whom those in full connection form the members of our conferences. These must be on trial for two years before they can be received into full connection with the conference, their character being examined at each conference (whether they be present or absent) in respect to moral, grace, gifts, and fruit. Nor can they be received upon trial as *travelling preachers,* till they have obtained a recommendation from the quarterly meetings of their respective circuits.[131]

"OF THE TRIAL OF THOSE WHO THINK THEY ARE MOVED BY THE HOLY GHOST TO PREACH":

We have enlarged on the present subject in our notes on the eighth section of this chapter [the one just excerpted above]. Every reader may from hence perceive the care we take in receiving our preachers and ministers. As the presiding elders, or those who have the charge of circuits, are attentive to the examination of the local preachers and exhorters, so the yearly conferences are attentive to the gifts, grace, and usefulness of all travelling preachers and ministers. Nothing will do for us without the *life of God.* Brilliant parts, fine addresses, &c. are to us but tinkling cymbals, when destitute of the power of the Holy Ghost.

At the same time we are far from despising *talents* which may be rendered useful to the church of Christ. We know the worth of improved abilities: and nothing can equal our itinerant plan, in the opportunity it affords of suiting our various societies with men of God, who are endued with gifts agreeable to their respective wants.[132]

SPIRITUAL DIRECTION UNDER "MOTHERS-IN-ISRAEL":

[Note an instance of the formative spiritual direction and perhaps two "mother-in-Israel" relationships described by Henry Boehm:]

"Harry Ennall's wife was one of the best of women. She was a Goldsbury, related to Governor Goldsbury. This was one of the great families of the Peninsula. They had no children, and always made the preachers very welcome. Mrs. Ennalls, who was a person of discernment, saw I was suffering under deep depression of spirits. I was fearful I had mistaken my calling. Ingenuously she asked me a great many questions, till she drew from me the real state of my mind. When she found out that I was discouraged, and about to give up my work in despair and return home, she gave me such a reproof as I shall never forget. 'My young brother,' she said, 'your eternal salvation may depend upon the course you are about to take. You may lose your soul by such an unwise, hasty step.' Then she exhorted me in the most earnest and emphatic manner not to abandon my work, but to keep on. I resolved in the strength of my Master to try again, and though over threescore years have gone into eternity since 'having obtained help from God, I continue unto this day.' Well I remember that hospitable mansion; and the room in which we were, the attitude of the woman, her anxious countenance, her piercing eye, the tone of her voice, are all before me just as if it were yesterday. Her wise counsel has had an influence upon me all my days; it shaped my destiny for life. She has been in the grave for many years, and I remember her still with a heart overflowing with gratitude.

"I then went to that famous house . . . where the widow of Squire Airey resided . . ."

[A footnote indicates that Boehm continued to stay with Mrs. Ennalls when she remarried after the death of her first husband.][133]

WILLIAM COLBERT ["SEMINARY OF THE ROAD" ENTRIES ONLY]:

[Baltimore] Dec. 30, 1790 spent some time in reading in the Arminian Magazine.

[next day] read the 6th Book of Milton's Paradise Lost. . . .

Jan. 17 [1791] read in the Bible at Elias Majors's and some of the Treatise of Christian Perfection. . . .

[next day] I spent some time in reading in Milton Paradise Lost. . . .

Thursday 20 read in the Bible. . . .

March, Saturday 26 I spent a considerable part of this day in reading in Dr. Limborch's Body of Divinity; and at night met a class at Wheeler's, and try'd to preach on the 10 virgins in Matt XXV. . . .

[May] Thursday 5 This morning set off with brother Ragan for conference in Baltimore; fell in with brother Andrew Nichols by the way . . . .

Friday 6 I appear'd in the conference gave in my experience, and was examin'd by the Bishop. At night heard John Dickins preach.

Saturday 7 I set in conference, and at night heard Ezekiel Cooper preach. Jonathan Forest gave an exhortation after him, he spoke with life and power.

Sunday 8 I rode about 15 miles, and preached at John Bonds on Matt. 22 & 14th with a degree of satisfaction and return'd to Baltimore at night and heard Bishop Asbury preach.

Monday 9 This morning I took breakfast with the Bishop and a great number of preachers at Philip Rogers, where our appointments were read out—Jeremiah Cosden and myself was appointed to Harford circuit . . . .

Sunday 29 . . . read in the Arminian Magazine

[June] Monday 20 I spent at Henry Warters' reading the Bible and Arminian Magazine.

[Sunday] 26 This morning I had to expel the class Leader in class meeting.

Thursday 30 . . . in the afternoon read in the Arminian Magazine of the wonderful work of God till I was happy. . . .

[Quarterly meeting at Pigmans Meeting House] sacrament was administer'd to a great number of souls.

Sunday 14 We had a very happy Love feast this morning, after which Ezekiel Cooper preached on John 9 &4 to, I don't know, but more people than I ever saw at any preaching before. Jonathan Forest and Nelson Reed exhorted after him. . . .

[Nov. 25–27 with Bishop Asbury visited college at Abingdon] . . .

[Dec.] Wednesday 7 I spent at Alexander Cooper's reading the Bible, Philosophy, Ovid Metromophieses, and writing.

[Christmas no special entry] . . .

[1792 January] Saturday 14 I spent at friend Homer's reading the sure guide to Hell, Wrote by Belzibub.

[July] Tuesday 10 read in the I of Vol. of Fletchers's works. . . .

Saturday 14 Spent at sister Taggerts where I got thro' the I Vol. of Fletcheres work's.

Wednesday August 1 Read in the II Vol. of Fletchere's works. . . .

Friday 24 Spent reading Aspasis Vindicated.

Saturday 25 I have got thro' Mr. Harvey's Book containing 450 pages. To me it has been like a long and tedious journey. It seems that I might compare myself to one (while reading) going thro' [sic] an enemies Land—traveling sword in hand: nevertheless, I think that this Book has been of use to me, giving me to see the subtility [sic] of calvinism.[134]

TESTIMONY AT EARLY UNITED BRETHREN ANNUAL CONFERENCES:[135]

September 25, 1800, the following preachers assembled at the house of Frederick Kemp in Frederick County, Maryland: William Otterbein, Martin Boehm, John Hershey, Abraham Troxel, Christian Krum, Henry Krum, George Pfrimmer, Henry Boehm, Christian Newcomer, Dietrich Aurand, Jacob Geisinger, George Adam Geeting, Adam Lehman.

Each person spoke first of his own experience, and then declared anew his intention with all zeal, through the help of God, to preach untrammeled by sect to the honor of God and [the good] of men. . . .

September 23, 1801, we again assembled at Peter Kemp's in order to counsel together and instruct one another how we might be pleasing to God and useful to our fellow men.

The following preachers were present: William Otterbein, Martin Boehm, Christian Newcomer, Daniel Strickler, George Adam Geeting, Peter Senseny, John Neidig, David Long, Abraham Mayer, Frederick Schaffer, Jacob Geisinger, John Hershey, Thomas Winter, Ludwig Duckwald, David Snyder, Peter Kemp, Matthias Kessler, Christian Krum, Abraham Hershey, Michael Thomas.

1. After prayer, Otterbein gave a discourse. He said that salvation depends on Christ alone and his mercy, and that whoever here becomes free from sin and a party spirit has God to thank. Thus he declared his mind, and then each of the preachers spoke of his experience, and then was the following resolved.

. . .

1. The 24th of September, 1801, we again assembled in God's name in Peter Kemp's house; and first a chapter of the Revelation of John was read, namely, the fourteenth chapter. Then followed singing and hearty prayer that each one might be willing to preach the gospel and that he also be careful, and that he also so walk as he preaches to others.

2. The preachers were examined as to whether they are willing according to their ability to labor in the work of the Lord, through the grace of the Lord.

. . .

5. Resolved that the preachers shall be brief and avoid unnecessary words in preaching and in prayer; but if the Spirit of God impels, it is their duty to follow as God directs. O God, give us wisdom and understanding to do all things according to thy will. Amen.

1. At nine o'clock we again came together. We began the session again with singing and hearty prayer that God would bless us with wisdom and understanding and with hearty love to God and one another. Amen. . . .

Martin Boehm.
William Otterbein.
George Adam Greeting.

At Cronise's, in Frederick County, [Maryland,] we, the following preachers, came together to hold counsel: William Otterbein, Martin Boehm, Christian Newcomer, John Hershey, Christopher Grosh, Abraham Troxel, Henry Krum, Michael Thomas, Dietrich Aurand, David Snyder, Peter Kemp, Matthias Kessler, George Adam Geeting.

We began our meeting with singing, then with right hearty prayer to God that the kingdom of God might come and the will of God be done on earth as in heaven. May God will to send us preachers the grace of love to love God and all men. . . .

2. Each of the preachers spoke of his condition, how it is with him in his preaching and how his purpose is further to do in his office, to call heartily upon God for his help, and that ever he might through humility give to another higher esteem than to himself. May God give to us preachers grace that we may become very humble to the honor of God and the good of men. . . .

14. Resolved that George Adam Geeting in the spring and fall shall visit the societies on Frederick Circuit.

15. Resolved that Christian Newcomer visit Cumberland Circuit twice yearly.

16. Resolved that Martin Boehm twice yearly visit the circuits in Pennsylvania

beyond the Susquehanna, to ascertain the condition of things in their societies.
. . .

18. Further, it is laid down as a rule [vest gesetzt] that when one of our superintendents [or elders, eltesten] dies, namely Otterbein or Martin Boehm, who now are appointed to the place [gesetzt sind], then shall another always be chosen in his stead. This is the wish of both, and all of the preachers present unanimously consent and are agreed that it be thus.

Now for this time is the session closed in God's name.

Martin Boehm.
William Otterbein.

1. October 5, 1803, as assembled at David Snyder's in Cumberland County, Pennsylvania. The preachers present were the following: William Otterbein, Martin Boehm, Christian Newcomer, Daniel Snyder, John Hershey, Peter Kemp, Abraham Mayer, Christopher Grosh, Christian Krum, Valentine Flugle, John Winter, Frederick Shaffer, George Adam Geeting, George Benedum.

We began the session with the reading of the second chapter of First Timothy, and then with singing some verses of a hymn, and with prayer. Thou, dear Savior, bless our coming together to the honor of thy name and to the edification of us all. O Lord, answer us for Jesus' sake. Amen.

2. Each one of the preachers spoke as to his condition, how it stood with him; and of his renewed determination in upright love with all, with earnest determination in uprightness toward one another, and bound together in love, to walk in the ways of God; to preach the gospel through the power of Jesus. Amen.

Wm. Otterbein.
Martin Boehm.
George Adam Geeting.

October 3, 1804, the conference met at David Snyder's. Few preachers came, however, on account of the prevailing sickness and mortality. Present, Christian Newcomer, Martin Boehm, Frederick Schaffer, David Snyder, Matthias Bortsfield.

They counseled together and resolved, the Lord willing, that the next conference be held near Middletown, Maryland, on Wednesday before Whitsunday, 1805.

1. May 29, 1805, we, the following preachers, assembled at the house of

Christian Newcomer. Both our [superintendents] were present—Otterbein and Boehm. John Hershey, George Adam Geeting, Daniel Strickler, Frederick Schaffer, Peter Kemp, Lorenz Eberhart, George Benedum, David Snyder, Christian Krum, Frederick Duckwald, William Ambrose, Jacob Baulus, Jacob Geisinger, Christian Berger, Abraham Mayer, Christian Newcomer.

2. We began the session with hearty prayer. Otterbein gave a short address. May the Lord Jesus grant his blessing to the same. Amen.

3. The assembled preachers resolved through the grace of Jesus Christ to urge forward the work of God with more earnestness than ever before. O dear Saviour, help us, poor and unworthy, for the sake of thy suffering and death. Amen. . . .

14. With this the session was brought to a close after the reading of a chapter and an exhortation that we should live to the honor of God.

William Otterbein.
Martin Boehm.

May 21, 1806, we held our conference for this year at Lorenz Eberhart's. The following preachers were present: John Neidig, Lorenz Eberhart, Joseph Hoffman, Peter Kemp, Christian Krum, Michael Thomas, John Hershey, Christian Newcomer, Jacob Baulus, Henry Krum, George Adam Geeting. O God, make thy servants very faithful.

2. Each preacher present spoke of his condition, how he stands with God, how it goes with him in his office, and his purpose henceforth to be faithful through our Jesus Christ.

3. On the 22nd of May we came together again. The question arose whether the preachers stand united in love. They all declared that they stand in hearty love, not only with one another, but also toward all men, whoever they may be. . . .

7. Great meetings shall be held at the school-house on the Antietam on Whitsunday, 1807; at Lemaster's, June 15; at the Spring [Rocky Spring], June 22; at Baulus's, October 4 and 5; at Hohmann's, in Virginia, September 24 and 25. The good Jesus bless his work. Amen.

George Adam Geeting.
Christian Newcomer.

1. We held our conference May 13, 1807, at Christian Herr's in Pennsylvania. The following preachers were present: Martin Boehm, Christian Newcomer, David Snyder, Isaac Niswander, Abraham Mayer, Christian Krum, John

Neidig, Frederick Schaffer, Christian Smith, Joseph Hoffman, George Adam Geeting, David Long, Christian Hershey, Abraham Hershey.

2. The session was opened with prayer; then every one spoke of his condition; afterward Brother Martin Boehm gave a short exhortation. The fourth chapter of First John was read. Would God that he would make of us all useful instruments. . . .

10. Resolved that our conference in 1808 shall be in Virginia, at Abraham Niswander's, Wednesday before the third Sunday in May.

Martin Boehm.
George Adam Geeting.

Stage 2: Collegial

COKE AND ASBURY COMMENTING "OF THE DUTIES OF THOSE WHO HAVE THE CHARGE OF CIRCUITS":

The person who holds it [the circuit], is to watch over the other traveling preachers in his circuit, not with the eye of severe judge, but with that of a tender elder brother. He should indeed be faithful to his colleagues, and tell them all their faults: but he has no power to correct them. He is to bear an equal share with them in the toils of a travelling preacher, besides having upon him the care of all the churches in his circuit. But if his colleagues will not observe his reasonable direction, or behave grossly amiss, he must inform his presiding elder, whose duty it is, as soon as possible, to judge of and rectify every thing.[136]

ROBERT PAINE ON WILLIAM McKENDREE'S YOKEFELLOW RELATIONS:

James O'Kelly was his first Presiding Elder, and Philip Cox, who had the charge of the circuit, was his first colleague. Mr. Cox seems to have been an excellent man, and proved a great blessing to his less experienced associate. His piety, prudence, amiability, and perseverance were of inestimable importance in forming the habits and molding the character of his junior brother. He was fortunate also in having his first year's work among such a community as he found on Mecklenburg Circuit. The prominent members of the Church sympathized with him, esteemed him highly, and sustained him by their counsels and their prayers. His fears and doubts began gradually to subside. The conviction deepened in his mind that to preach the gospel was essential to his own happiness; and as he was constrained to believe that his efforts were crowned with the blessing of God in the conversion of souls, his feelings became much relieved as to his duty before the year closed.[137]

ELIJAH HEDDING'S BIOGRAPHER REPORTING ON THE RELATION OF HEDDING TO DAN YOUNG:

At the close of this conference Mr. Hedding was appointed to the Barre Circuit, in Vermont. This circuit lay nearly in the middle of the state, and extended over thirteen towns, including Montpelier, the present capital of the state. Mr. Hedding had for his colleague the Rev. Dan Young. Of him he says: "He was a young man of superior talents, and of great piety and zeal. He travelled a few years, and laboured with great success on other circuits afterward. He then located, and lived a few years in New-Hampshire; and then became a member of the state senate. Afterward he removed to Ohio. We laboured together with great comfort, and were happy in our own souls in the love of God, and saw the people happy under our ministry."

The hearts of these young men were knit together like those of David and Jonathan. They entered into a mutual agreement to aid each other in mental and religious improvement. They adjusted their work so that once a fortnight they would meet in the middle of the circuit, on a week day, and preach in each other's presence—one in the afternoon and the other in the evening. "We agreed," says Mr. Hedding, "to tell each other all the faults we discovered in our preaching—either in doctrine, pronunciation, gesture, or otherwise. We next agreed to tell each other all the faults we discovered in private life, and all that we feared of each other; and then we agreed to tell all we heard, and all the people said of each other. This mutual agreement was the source of much profit to us, and we continued to practise it to the end of the year; nor was it the occasion of any ill feeling between us." Nothing can more strikingly attest the desire of these young men to improve themselves in all that pertains to a workman that needeth not to be ashamed; nothing can more finely illustrate the confidence they had in each other, and the mutual affection that subsisted between them.[138]

COMMENT BY AN UNIDENTIFIED COLLEAGUE OF WILLIAM WRIGHT:

I met our dear brother on Annamessex Circuit in the month of May last, and found him much devoted to God and his work. We labored together for more than three months; during which time we met every two weeks, and, as was our custom, gave each other a relation of our particular exercises and state of the circuit.[139]

PETER CARTWRIGHT ON COLLEGIAL FORMATION:

We had at this early day no course of study prescribed, as at present; but William M'Kendree, afterward bishop, but then my presiding elder, directed me to a proper course of reading and study. He selected books for me, both literary and theological; and every quarterly visit he made, he examined into my progress, and corrected my errors, if I had fallen into any. He delighted to instruct me in English grammar.

Brother Lakin had charge of the circuit. My business was to preach, meet the classes, visit the society and the sick, and then to my books and study; and I say that I am more indebted to Bishop M'Kendree for my little attainments in literature and divinity, than to any other man on earth. And I believe that if presiding elders would do their duty by young men in this way, it would be more advantageous than all the colleges and Biblical institutes in the land; for they then could learn and practice every day. Suppose, now, Mr. Wesley had been obliged to wait for a literary and theologically trained band of preachers before he moved in the glorious work of his day, what would Methodism have been in the Wesleyan connection to-day? Suppose the Methodist Episcopal Church in these United States had been under the necessity of waiting for men thus qualified, what would her condition have been at this time? In despite of all John Wesley's prejudices, he providentially saw that to accomplish the glorious work for which God had raised him up, he must yield to the superior wisdom of Jehovah, and send out his "lay preachers" to wake up a slumbering world. If Bishop Asbury had waited for this choice literary band of preachers, infidelity would have swept these United States from one end to the other. Methodism in Europe this day would have been as a thousand to one, if the Wesleyans had stood by the old land-marks of John Wesley: but no; they must introduce pews, literary institutions and theological institutes, till a plain, old-fashioned preacher, such as one of Mr. Wesley's "lay preachers," would be scouted, and not allowed to occupy one of their pulpits. Some of the best and most useful men that were ever called of God to plant Methodism in this happy republic were among the early pioneer preachers, east, west, north, and south; and especially in our mighty West. We have no such preachers now as some of the first ones who were sent out to Kentucky and Tennessee.

The Presbyterians, and other Calvinistic branches of the Protestant Church, used to contend for an educated ministry, for pews, for instrumental music, for a congregational or stated salaried ministry. The Methodists universally opposed these ideas; and the illiterate Methodist preachers actually set the world on fire, (the American world at least,) while they were lighting their matches![140]

WILLIAM F. WARREN, SOON-TO-BE PRESIDENT OF BOSTON UNIVERSITY, ON THE COLLEGIAL PATTERN OF FORMATION, ITS PASSING, AND THE COURSE OF STUDY:

About a generation ago a great change occurred in the practical working of our ecclesiastical system. Through all the older and more settled portions of the Church the circuit system was generally abandoned. The gravity of this change has seldom, if ever, been duly estimated. Measured by its effects upon the whole Church, it is entitled to be designated a radical revolution.

The first and most serious result of this revolution was the practical paralysis of our whole system of ministerial training. The great theological seminary of Methodism was not indeed closed, but it received a blow equivalent to that which would be dealt to a college by abolishing its working faculty. . . .

It effectively deprived our candidates and junior ministry of the instruction, drill, and personal influence which they had been wont to receive from their senior associates upon the district and the circuit. It robbed them of the stimulus and profit of contact with superior minds, the advantages of living models, the blessed contagion of maturer character."

WILLIAM WARREN ON THE COURSE OF STUDY:

There is in this country one theological school of special interest. It is the largest in the world. Its last Freshman class numbered seven hundred and ninety-three. The entire number of students now in attendance is about three thousand. While other theological institutions, the world over, have required but a brief three years' course of study, this one has from the beginning prescribed four years. While other seminaries surrender a quarter of the year for vacation, this one is in uninterrupted operation from one year's end to the other. . . . Its alumni, living and dead, are numbered by tens of thousands. Its campus is broader than the continent.

[Its "fundamental principles," he asserted were,]

1. "It is based upon the idea *that the professional instruction and training of the ministry ought to be in the hands of the Church.*"

2. "The system adopted by our fathers *proposed to train for the ministry no man whom God had not called to the ministry.*" It "demanded . . . provision for legitimate ecclesiastical control," "affirmed the essential freedom of the human soul, and jealously guarded responsible personal agency." It "demanded . . . that it restrict itself to legitimate subjects; that is, to those who have been called of God to the work of the ministry, and whose divine call has been accepted and ratified by the individual and the Church."

3. "The system inaugurated by our fathers *provided for a happy blending of the theoretical and practical in ministerial education.*"[141]

Stage 3: Conferenced

THE 1816 GENERAL CONFERENCE ON THE IMPORTANCE OF STUDY:

Although a collegiate education is not, by your committee, deemed essential to a gospel ministry, yet it appears absolutely necessary for every minister of the gospel to study to show himself approved unto God, a workman that needeth not to be ashamed. Every one, therefore, who would be useful as a minister in the Church, should, to a sincere piety and laudable zeal for the salvation of souls, add an ardent desire for useful knowledge—he should strive by every lawful means to imbue his mind with every science which is intimately connected with the doctrine of salvation by Jesus Christ, and which will enable him to understand and illustrate the sacred Scriptures.[142]

THE COURSE OF STUDY—1817:

The Holy Ghost saith, "Study to shew thyself approved unto God, a workman that needeth not be ashamed: right dividing the word of Truth"— To this end the preacher should be sufficiently acquainted with the depravity of the human heart—Redemption by Christ—Repentance towards God—Justification by faith in our Lord Jesus Christ, who is very and Eternal God—The direct Witness of the Spirit—Holiness of heart and Life, and also the doctrine of Perseverance—The Resurrection of the dead and future Rewards and Punishments.

To enforce these doctrines with propriety the teacher must be conversant with Scriptures in general, and with Geography and History.

The art of conveying ideas with ease, propriety and clearness is of great importance. The Candidate should understand the Articles of Religion, and the doctrines and discipline of the Church, to which he is to subscribe, and by which he is to be governed

1st On Divinity, a constant use of the Holy Scriptures. Wesley's Sermons—Notes—answer to Taylor—Saints Rest—Law's Serious Call—Benson's Sermons—Coke's Commentaries—Fletcher's Checks—Appeal—Portrait of Saint Paul—Wood's Dictionary—Newton on the Prophecies—and Wesley's Philosophy.

2nd Rollins' Ancient History, Josephus's Antiquities, with Wesley's Ecclesiastical History.

3rd. The Rudiments of the English language, Alexander's, Murray's, or Webster's Grammar.

4th. Morse's Universal and Paine's Geography.[143]

A REVIEW OF WATSON'S *THEOLOGICAL INSTITUTES* PRAISED THE TREATISE FOR ITS VALUE FOR PERSONS ON THE COURSE OF STUDY WHEN LATER ADDED:

We sincerely congratulate the author, and the persons for whose benefit the "Theological Institutes" were undertaken, on the completion of this work. Some of the junior ministers belonging to the Methodist body have enjoyed the advantages of a liberal education, and are well prepared by previous literary and theological study for the office which they sustain. Others of them, however, have not been thus favored. Their piety and natural talents will not be questioned by those who are acquainted with them, and their labours are justly esteemed by these who sit under their ministry; but they need greater assistance in the prosecution of their studies than has yet been given to them. Mr. Watson's work will be of great utility to them in several respects. It will assist them in forming an acquaintance with the entire system of Christianity: for those who "labour in the word and doctrine," should not confine their attention to any particular set of doctrines, but should diligently, and in the spirit of prayer, investigate the whole "truth as it is in Jesus." Called, with St. Paul to "declare the whole counsel of God," every minister of Christ should study the doctrines of religion in their connexion with each other, with the attributes of God, the spiritual privileges of believers, and the moral obligations of mankind. By this means only can the Christian scribe become "well instructed," and qualified to bring out of his treasury "things new and old," to the edification and comfort of the people who attend his ministrations. To say that the "Theological Institutes" are complete would be folly. Works of this nature are capable of amplification to an indefinite extent; and the ever varying forms of error call for new defenses of the truth; but we led ourselves fully justified in saying, there is no work of the same kind in the English language from which the persons for whose benefit it is intended can derive so much valuable instruction.[144]

LA ROY SUNDERLAND ON THE COURSE OF STUDY AND THEOLOGICAL EDUCATION:

The *Discipline* makes no provision for the conferences to point out a course of study for candidates on trial. All the *Discipline* authorizes is to be done by the bishops through the presiding elders. In many cases, however, nothing is done. The candidate never has any course of study pointed out by any one; at least, this has been the case, I know, in this conference. Lately, however, in the South Carolina, Philadelphia, Mississippi, Alabama, and Georgia conferences, a uniform system of study has been adopted, which candidates for deacon's and elder's orders are required to pursue; and according to which they are to be examined, it seems, once a year for four years successively. A similar course had been prepared and printed by a committee of the New-York conference, and approved of by the bishops, which has been used with good effect, I am informed, in that conference. It was afterward adopted by the New-England conference; but without any benefit, I believe, to any one, as it was never, to my knowledge, used to any extent in this conference, either by the candidates or the examining committee. Indeed, I presume, it never was used by the examining committee through the course of even one examination. But the course of study adopted by the conferences above named, and which has been published a number of times lately in the Christian Advocate and Journal, is generally considered, probably, as the highest and the very best course of study which, has ever been recommended, or required of candidates for membership in any of our conferences.

I have expressed the opinion before that this course of study is but limited— it is partial; and considering the nature of the sacred office, I do think it must appear to be extremely so, to any one who looks into the subject with attention. And how could it well be otherwise? The persons for whom these plans for study are recommended, it must be remembered, have already commenced the multifarious and arduous duties of the Gospel ministry, without any considerable knowledge of theology, and sometimes, perhaps, without any kind of an education whatever; so that about all they know, both of letters and divinity, they must pick up, after they have engaged in their pastoral labors—labors, which, under any circumstances, are enough, as every faithful minister knows, to require all the time, and patience, and attention, which any one can bestow.[145]

...Practical theology, it is said, embraces all the different branches of theological science which have reference to preaching; the multiplied ways in which the truths of the Gospel may be most successfully set home to the hearts and consciences of men; in a word, every thing relating to the theory of sacred eloquence, and the performance of every duty connected with the care of souls. Nor is this deficiency supplied in the additional works mentioned in the above course, which are "recommended," merely, to such as have leisure and means to study them.[146]

...It is as clear as the light of noon day, that, for the Methodist Episcopal Church to do her part toward evangelizing the world, she must advance in the education of her ministers. I say, if we mean to do our part of the work, which is due from the Church of God to the people of these United States, we must advance in the education of our ministers. This is a new country; the moral and intellectual habits of the people are yet, in no small degree, to be formed. This must be done by education, by sanctified learning. Matter is moved by mind. And who will furnish the reading and the influence which is to mould and fashion the general character of this great and growing people? Those ministers who take the lead in promoting the means and blessings of sanctified learning will wield the future destinies of this powerful nation.[147]

Stage 4: Collegiate

GENERAL CONFERENCE 1820 ON COLLEGES:

Almost all seminaries of learning [academies or colleges] in our country, of much celebrity, are under the control of Calvinistic or of Hopkinsian principles, or otherwise are managed by men denying the fundamental doctrines of the gospel. If any of our people, therefore, wish to give their sons or daughters a finished education, they are under the necessity of resigning them to the management of those institutions which are more or less hostile to our views of the grand doctrines of Christianity.

Another capital defect in most seminaries of learning, your committee presumes to think, is, that experimental and practical godliness is considered only of secondary importance; whereas, in the opinion of your committee, this ought to form the most prominent feature in every literary institution. Religion and learning should mutually assist each other, and thus connect the happiness of both worlds together.

General Conference then recommended that "all the annual conferences" establish "as soon as practicable literary institutions under their own control" and ordered that "a copy of this report be recorded on the journals of the several Annual Conferences."[148]

MINISTERIAL FORMATION AT WESLEYAN UNIVERSITY 1837:

"Dear and Much-beloved Parents, . . . We arrived, somewhat weary, at the university about seven, P. M. I am received as a member in a class of forty or more—the largest class they have ever had. I occupy room No. 12 in the college, with my former chum, Robert Allyn. I am much pleased with my situation. It is an interesting sight to behold such a number of young men as are here assembled, sixty or more of whom are members of the Methodist E. Church, and a great part of whom are preparing to preach the everlasting gospel. The Lord bless them.

"I have no time to lose—have employment for every moment. We attend prayers in the morning at six o'clock, in the chapel, immediately after which we repair to our respective recitation rooms; thence to breakfast; return to our rooms, and study until eleven, when we recite again; dine at twelve; exercise and study until five, P. M., when we have prayers again in the chapel; retire at ten in the evening; and thus passes the day, with other exercises which occur in their proper place. . . .

"30th. Some time has elapsed since I wrote last. I have, in the mean time, been closely engaged in my studies. Sabbath before last attended meeting in Middlefield, where a good revival has commenced. Meetings are held by brother Rosser, who is very much interested for the welfare of the people. I enjoyed myself while there for the most part well.

"O Lord, continue to revive thy work! How meagre [sic] this world, with all its charms, compared with the glories of heaven! Help me to realize this more fully, and act accordingly.

"I find that college is no place for idleness, but a place for application and constant effort. I have joined the society termed the Missionary Lyceum.[149] Last evening attended love-feast in the chapel—it was a good season. This day has nearly gone: how fast time flies! it is constantly bearing me to the tomb. May I wisely improve the passing privileges! . . . "

"My advantages in this place are great. The meetings which we attend on sabbath and during the week are the following: Sabbath, A. M., meeting in the college chapel, when either Dr. Fisk, or the chaplain. Rev. Prof. Holdich, preaches. In the afternoon attend church in the city, in the place of regular circuit preaching. At half-past five of the same day we have a prayer meeting in some one of the rooms of college. Wednesday evening, class meeting; Friday evening, prayer meeting; Saturday evening, band meeting, which to me, and I may say to all who attend, is the most profitable exercise. This evening have been much blessed in band.

"I have engaged a school for about three months in Rochester, Mass., near where cousin Franklin is stationed, to commence the first Monday in December. He formerly taught the same school."[150]

Stage 5: Seminary

PETER CARTWRIGHT QUESTIONS THE VALUE OF THEOLOGICAL EDUCATION:

Perhaps, among the thousands of traveling and local preachers employed and engaged in this glorious work of saving souls, and building up the Methodist Church, there were not fifty men that had anything more than a common

English education, and scores of them not that; and not one of them was ever trained in a theological school or Biblical institute, and yet hundreds of them preached the Gospel with more success and had more seals to their ministry than all the sapient, downy D.D.'s in modern times, who, instead of entering the great and wide-spread harvest-field of souls, sickle in hand, are seeking presidencies or professorships in colleges, editorships, or any agencies that have a fat salary, and are trying to create newfangled institutions where good livings can be monopolized, while millions of poor, dying sinners are thronging the way to hell without God, without Gospel; and the Church putting up the piteous wail about the scarcity of preachers.[151]

JAMES STRONG ADVOCATES "A CENTRAL THEOLOGICAL SEMINARY":

The demand for superior theological training in our Church shows itself in a two-fold form, arising from the upward tendency of Methodism, like many other successful and progressive principle, from the lower to the higher stratum of society. As our congregations increase in number and wealth, they naturally increase likewise in intelligence, either by a gradual improvement in the mental culture of the mass, or by the introduction among them of persons of more than ordinary learning and refinement. These congregations cannot now be satisfied with the quality of preaching, in a literary point of view, with which they once were.[152]

RANDOLPH S. FOSTER ON A MINISTRY "LEARNED" AND "CONSECRATED":

The Church needs a thoroughly-educated and liberally-informed ministry. . . . as including a thorough training to habits of study, and extensive cultivation in the entire circle of the sciences, and of all human knowledge, so far as practicable, bearing directly or remotely on theology. . . .Methodism needs a more spiritual and consecrated ministry.

We want prophets of the closet as well as study; men whose hearts glow while their intellects shine: who feel deeply, as well as think profoundly: who experience, as well as theorize: consecrated, as well as ordained: men, who walk with God and who are entrusted with his secrets: who go before the Church, and say, "Follow us as we follow Christ. . . ."

Is any one about to say, The thing can never be: a ministry of this kind? A ministry so learned, and yet so consecrated; so intellectual, and yet so spiritual; so much culture, and yet so great zeal. Why not? Has history recorded no examples? Have the instances been few of great learning, and yet great devotion? Count up the heroes of the Church, and what do you find? Whence have come the great lights, whose names gleam on the martyrs' page, and reformers' roll? Who are they who have braved kings and senates, and who paled not at the stake and wheel And why not? Is education a foe to religion? Is enlargement of the intellect inimical to devoutness of the heart? Are they who are best capable to understand the truth, and who take in more of its effulgence, less likely to be faithful to it, to love it and with zeal to propagate it? Surely these things cannot be a necessity. To believe so for a moment would extinguish our lights of hope for the future, and overthrow our faith in the history of the past. The things are not irreconcilable. Light and heat do blend in the same beam; and so wisdom and love animate the same soul, and spread their effulgence and power over the same ministry.

We must have it: culture and zeal, light and heat, mind and heart! Blended, they will give us power with men and power with God, and we shall prevail. Deprived of them, we shall sink down, down, down in weakness and imbecility, until not a historic vestige will be left of a people who might have been great for God in the earth.[153]

A REVIEW OF FOSTER'S EFFORT ATTEMPTED TO SMOKE OUT HIS INTENT:

Dr. Foster's first proposition is that the "Church needs a thoroughly-educated and liberally-informed ministry"; the second, that she needs "a more spiritual and consecrated ministry." With positions thus stated no one could find fault; but when Dr. Foster comes to set them forth in detail, he gets upon debatable ground. It is to be regretted that Dr. Foster does not accurately define what he means by a thoroughly-educated ministry. If it be his purpose to advocate an absolute requisition of liberal training (say in college and in the Theological Seminary) from all candidates for the ministry, he has failed signally, and will always fail in accomplishing it. If, on the other hand, he means simply to assert that the Church should furnish the amplest means of culture for such of her young men as may have the opportunity to make use of them, he will find few to dispute with him. But the whole tenor of his argument seems to imply the former doctrine; and, for this reason, the discourse, though abounding in earnest and urgent appeals, which, if put forth simply with a view to stimulate our candidates and younger ministers to more enlarged and liberal studies, would be signally efficacious and useful, will now, we fear, only excite an opposition, to which his broad and often unguarded statements lay him abundantly open.[154]

THE 1892 GENERAL CONFERENCE ON THE UNIVERSITY SENATE AND MEC EDUCATIONAL INSTITUTIONS:

Report No. II Committee on Education concerning "The Board of Education":

9. The educational institutions under the patronage of the Methodist Episcopal Church shall be classified as follows: (1) Primary schools; (2) Secondary schools; (3) Colleges; (4) Universities; (5) Schools of Theology. . . .

13. Theological schools whose professors are nominated or confirmed by the Bishops exist for the benefit of the whole Church. It is the duty of the Bishops, presiding elders, and pastors to direct the attention of our young people to our literary institutions, and the candidates for our ministry, having proper qualifications, to our theological seminaries.

14. There shall be a University Senate of the Methodist Episcopal Church, authorized by the General Conference and appointed by the Board of Bishops, composed of practical educators, one from each General Conference District and one at large, who shall determine the minimum equivalent of academic work in our Church institutions for graduation to the Baccalaureate degree. The curricula thus determined shall provide for the historical and literary study of the Bible in the vernacular.

15. The Senate shall at least quadrennially report to the Board of Education its work; and that Board shall determine the institutions which meet these requirements, and such institutions shall be designated as colleges in the official lists of the educational institutions of the Church.[155]

FRANKLIN C. WOODWARD OF WOFFORD COLLEGE ON THE INADEQUACIES OF THE COURSE OF STUDY AND THE NECESSITY OF A COLLEGE EDUCATION FOR MINISTRY:

The tests are made "far too easy." "There is," he insisted, "probably no learned profession to which access is so free."

[A] man may enter the itinerant ranks without giving to preparation for his great work as much time and pains as would be required to make him a good journeyman carpenter! Numbers do enter and remain in it who would hardly make ordinarily useful laymen—men without the mere rudiments of a sound education, ignorant of the world's thought and progress, of science and literature, of Methodist doctrine and polity, of theology and Church history; men who have no love of reading and study, and who do neither—who cannot read understandingly the Book they pretend to teach, who cannot write a correct complex sentence, or understand it when written; men, moreover, who would not be thus burdening the Church and demoralizing its ministry if a moderately fair test had been applied in their admission. . . .

It is useless to hope this class of preachers will fit themselves for work in the midst of work. The itinerancy is a fine field for trained laborers, but a bad place for crude apprentices. . . . to the man void of literary resources self-education is almost an impossibility. . . .

Not only does the door stand too wide open: there is injudicious zeal in inviting entrance. The average boy—most applicants may be so classed—newly converted, ardent in his love of Christ, eager to do something in his cause, seeking opportunity to show his zeal, sometimes—often, indeed—it is to be feared, mistakes his unanalyzed emotions of gratitude and love for a call to preach. . . .

Unfortunately, the call to preach is not understood to be a "call to prepare," but rather as an equivalent for preparation. . . .

The Methodist ministry is the paradise of ease-loving indolence, the refuge of secular failures. . . .

It is too much to ask of cultivated men and women to listen patiently Sunday after Sunday, month after month, year after year, to solecism, historical blunders, false exegesis, worn-out arguments, travesties of the gospel, caricatures of truth! . . .

It would not be demanding too much of applicants for this high calling to insist upon their taking a thorough collegiate course.[156]

THE 1897 PHILADELPHIA COURSE OF STUDY:

The examinations will be written or oral, or both, at the option of the Board of Examiners.

For the "books to be read" the examiner will require a syllabus of each book, and will expect said syllabus not only to give an analysis of the work, but also to show that the contents of the book have been mastered by the candidate, and the examiners shall decide upon and report upon the syllabi as satisfactory or not satisfactory.

Written sermons are to be presented at or sent in before the June examination, as should be all syllabi assigned to that date. Exegetical studies should be sent in prior to the December examination, as should be all syllabi belonging to the same period. Essays and other syllabi should be sent in on or before the first of February, 1898.

All candidates will be required to pursue the course of study and to pass the examinations thereon.

Those examined "shall be graded upon the scale of 100, and none below 70 per cent. shall pass." (Appendix to *Discipline*, 57.)

It is hoped that during the evenings of the days on which the examinations shall occur, and at certain hours during the day time, special lectures may be delivered by persons eminent in various departments of theological and church work.

Members of the several classes are recommended to attend, as far as practicable, the Ministerial Institute.

[In June, the first year class was to be examined on John Miley's *Systematic Theology* 1: 1–266, Henry Martyn Harman's *Introduction to the Holy Scriptures*, 1–109, Charles Horswell's *Suggestions for the Study of the English New Testament*, a written sermon, and a syllabus on William Arthur's *Tongue of Fire*.

In December that class was responsible for the rest of Miley 1, Harman, 109-447, Adam S. Hill's *Principles of Rhetoric*, to undertake exegetical studies in the Gospels, and to produce syllabi on Thomas Neely's *Governing Conference in Methodism* and John Wesley's *Sermons 2*.

At the annual conference examination, the first year had responsibility for George Park Fisher's *Outlines of Universal History*, John Wesley's *Plain Account of Christian Perfection*, James Buckley's *Theory and Practice of Extemporaneous Preaching*, an essay with syllabi of William W. Martin's *Ecclesiastical Architecture* and Daniel Dorchester's *Problem of Religious Progress*.]

THE MEC BISHOPS ON PREPARATION FOR MINISTRY 1896:

The MEC bishops had counseled and General Conference had made provision for certificates to satisfy the examination requirement in 1896. The bishops affirmed:

"The conditions of admitting preachers to our Conferences are based on a state of things that existed many years ago, when circumstances were very different. Our whole system has been based on gifts, graces, and usefulness developed by a course of study pursued amid the difficulties of regular work by junior preachers under a senior. As a regular drill in practical work it could not be easily surpassed. But it is not now practicable to so relate junior and senior preachers, and the course of study is much better pursued in our colleges and theological seminaries. . . . We believe the time has fully come when the Church should recognize in the conditions to admission on trial to our Conferences the preparation gained in the theological schools. The Church has already advanced one step in this direction by ordaining as deacons those who have been local preachers, have been students for two years in one of our regular theological seminaries, and have completed the first two years of the Conference Course of Study. We now recommend that the Church take one more step in advance and enact that any student shall be credited on the Conference Course of Study with examination in any of the books of the first two years of the Conference Course which any theological school, whose professors are nominated and confirmed by the bishops, shall certify that he has satisfactorily passed."[157]

Stage 6: Synthesized

ROBERT KELLY FROM *Theological Education in America:*

This study grew out of the widely-held belief that the machinery and the methods used in educating Protestant ministers were inadequate. It was asserted that the number and the quality of ministerial candidates had been on the decline for some time and that the churches faced a crisis because of the real or the prospective dearth of leaders. . . .

The expansion of the field of pastoral theology is conspicuous in the Methodist Episcopal group. Their programs propose to relate the church to the present social order. They provide numerous courses in religious education; psychology of religion; practical survey methods, both for church and community; sociology; social service; city church; rural church; clinical work, etc. Garrett and Boston are particularly strong in these regards. . . .

No group of denominational seminaries is making a more strenuous effort to apply thorough scientific methods to the training of preachers who are to become social engineers and religious educators.[158]

WILLIAM ADAMS BROWN AND MARK MAY FROM *The Education of American Ministers:*[159]

THE MOST IMPORTANT CHANGES

The most important changes that have taken place in theological curricula during the past twenty-five or thirty years have been four in number. They have been due (1) to the enlargement in the subject matter to be taught; (2) to the increasing provision for election; (3) to the provision, in certain institutions, for preparation for a differentiated ministry; (4) to changes in educational theory which extend the seminary's responsibility beyond that which is taught in the classroom and put emphasis on what the student learns by doing. A word as to each: . . .

(4) We note finally a growing tendency toward a more enlarged conception of the curriculum—a conception which goes beyond the course of study and includes all sorts of cultural and educational experiences which the seminary and the community provide. This tendency is reinforced by the growing

emphasis in educational circles upon the educational value of practice as a key to knowledge. We learn by doing; and the older view of the curriculum as a body of knowledge to be mastered for its own sake is attacked in many quarters as inadequate if not positively false.[160]

[Later in that chapter they dealt with two emerging issues:]

Professional vs. Vocational Training: One of these issues is the distinction between vocational and professional education. This is not to be confused with the distinction between functional education and that which has for its primary aim the acquisition of a body of knowledge for its own sake. All true professional education is functional. It is rather the distinction between the type of education that aims to furnish a man with the type of training required by all ministers, and that which trains for a specialized ministry. It corresponds in medicine to the distinction between the general practitioner and the specialist; and in engineering, to the distinction between trade schools, which are vocational, and engineering schools, which are professional. The vocational school gives the student specific skills in the details of the task he is to perform; the professional school attempts to give him a broad foundation of principles and skill in thinking out practical problems, with the belief that he will acquire the special practical skills when he gets on the job. . . .

The curricula of most seminaries are obvious compromises between the vocational and the professional view. Even where the vocational view is consciously adopted, many seminaries seem to be limiting themselves to the kinds of practical skill that can be developed in the classroom. A few, to be sure, are making place for laboratory or clinical work in parishes, Sunday schools, etc. This movement, of great educational importance, is discussed fully in the chapter on field work. In the courses designed to prepare for the more basic activities common to all forms of the profession, the emphasis seems to be on the mastery of subject-matter rather than skill in the use of it. The Bible in its original languages is gradually being replaced by a knowledge of the conclusions reached by men who possess this skill.

Content and Skill: This brings us to a second fundamental educational issue. Stated briefly, it is whether or not the curriculum shall be viewed as a body of subject-matter, done up in course packages to be dealt out to and digested by the students, or is it to be viewed as an orderly series of experiences arranged to achieve definite goals. According to the first view, the seminary is a place where the student gets information; according to the second, it is a place where he has educational experiences, only part of which are derived from books. The issue is not so much in the nature of an antithesis as it is a narrower or broader view of the curriculum. The narrower view regards the curriculum primarily as a course of study, the major experiences being book and classroom contacts with teachers; the broader view regards the curriculum as including all educational experiences of the student.

The broader view is easy to take, but hard to carry out in practice. Most seminaries will tell us they subscribe to the broader view; but their curricula are built on the narrower one. The difficulty is that there are so many truly educational experiences that cannot be catalogued and reduced to courses and credit hours. The alumni of any seminary will give eloquent testimony to the fact that some of the greatest benefits derived from their seminary life came from experiences not included in the curriculum. Why, it may plausibly be asked, should we not leave them there—as experiences of the student's free personality reacting naturally to the ordinary contacts of life? Why organize and classify and institutionalize them? Here we come upon the outstanding weakness in American higher education. It is course-minded, and credit-minded. Things that cannot somehow be squeezed into the system of courses and credits do not get in. We proceed on the theory that learning is getting information; and that information is contained in books and lectures which can be classified into courses and properly labeled. Getting an education is, externally at least, a process of passing courses, and rolling up a score of credits which at the end of a specified time can be cashed in for a degree.

The seminaries are not the only institutions in the course business. The curricula of secondary schools, colleges, professional and graduate schools are built on the same general plan. The indictment, if it is to be made, must be against the whole American system. Whether the seminaries alone can break free from it is an open question. There is encouraging evidence that some of them are trying to do this. The matter of field work already referred to is a case in point. . . .[161]

[Brown and May concluded their detailed survey of the various designs for field education with this appraisal:]

This review of significant experiments in progress must indicate the vitality of the movement to make supervised field work a fully integrated aspect of theological education. Indeed the evidences of effective field work presented in this chapter and the indications of its rapid extension, might with reason lead to the conclusion that supervised, graded experience as the core around which curriculum courses are formed, will soon be considered as essential to an adequate training for the ministry as it is now considered necessary to an adequate training for engineering, for law, and for medicine.[162]

JOHN O. GROSS in 1960:

The past twenty-five years have witnessed the greatest period of growth for our theological schools. The B.D degree has become the basis for admission to the itinerant ministry. This past year 82 per cent of all persons received into full connection were graduates of theological seminaries. In the past decade enrollments in our seminaries have increased 87 per cent. By 1970 the number of men studying in our theological schools should reach five thousand.

Today the atmosphere in our church is more congenial for theological schools than ever before.[163]

Stage 7: Contextualized

THEOLOGICAL EDUCATORS AND THE BISHOPS OUTLINE:

"A Wesleyan Vision for Theological Education and Leadership Formation for the 21st Century"[164]

THE COUNCIL OF BISHOPS ENTERTAINS ITS OWN VISION FOR THEOLOGICAL EDUCATION AND LEADERSHIP FORMATION:

Leading Into the Future
A Report of the Task Force on
Theological Education and Leadership Formation
To the Council of Bishops, May 5, 2011

The United Methodist Church is at a critical moment in its history where its present structures and approaches stand in need of reform. Part of that change is a greater investment in the future of the church's life and mission. . . . [T]he most important investment that could be made is in developing the church's leadership.

The UMC needs theological education that prepares women and men for leadership in making disciples of Jesus Christ for the transformation of the world. (See the appendix "What Kind of Theological Education Do We Need?") This education will be rooted in Wesleyan understandings, practices, and ethos and will be shaped by a missional identity. Evidence of its effectiveness will be seen in the fruitfulness of the work of its graduates. We recognize that theological education may take many forms, and we encourage theological schools and others to experiment and to look for creative models around the world that might be fitting and fruitful for their own contexts and for the mission of the church. Specifically, we know as a worldwide church

126

that we must give attention to theological education in Central Conferences and Mission areas and provide more adequate funding patterns and partnerships that will enrich theological education in all places. We also know that the institutions of theological education need both greater support and greater accountability.

In "A Wesleyan Vision for Theological Education and Leadership Formation" (www.gbhem.org) the Council of Bishops affirmed six calls. Not only are these calls still valid, but we have only begun to realize the vision embodied in them. Specifically, we affirm that the church's agenda still includes the following:

1. We call upon the Church to develop strategies to identify and assess, articulate and embody, nurture and sustain pastoral excellence that is faithful and effective in shaping communities that are signs, foretastes, and instruments of God's reign.

2. We call upon the Church to develop a commitment to catechesis for all Christians, especially through attention to the distinctive witness of our Wesleyan tradition.

3. We call upon the Church to emphasize and reinvigorate its financial, institutional, and programmatic support and accountability for the networks that prepare laity and clergy alike for leadership roles in the Church.

4. We call upon the Church to develop a more clearly articulated, widely understood, and coherent theology of ordination that identifies the distinctive yet complementary roles of laity and clergy.

5. We call upon the Church to commit to strengthening the relationships among all those bodies that are crucial for calling forth, educating and equipping, and deploying leaders in the Church.

6. We call upon the Church, through the leadership of the Council of Bishops and with assistance from relevant bodies, to develop a comprehensive plan for the funding of theological education and leadership formation in The United Methodist Church.

. . .

COUNCIL OF BISHOPS TASK FORCE ON THEOLOGICAL EDUCATION AND LEADERSHIP FORMATION

WHAT KIND OF THEOLOGICAL EDUCATION DO WE NEED?
Working Document from the Council of Bishops Task Force on Theological Education and Leadership Formation, April, 2010

What kind of theological education does The United Methodist Church need to develop principled Christian leadership?

The UMC needs theological education that prepares women and men for leadership in making disciples of Jesus Christ for the transformation of the world. This education will be rooted in Wesleyan understandings, practices, and ethos and will be shaped by a missional identity. Evidence of its effectiveness will be seen in the graces, gifts, and fruit of its graduates.

We recognize that theological education may take many forms, and we encourage theological schools and others to experiment and to look for creative models around the world that might be fitting and fruitful for their own contexts and for the mission of the church.

Whatever the models, those who engage in theological education will develop a practice of life-long learning and growth in Christ. Such education begins with ongoing conversion and transformation of the self. Key components of this education will include:

1. Knowledge: forming and nurturing leaders with knowledge rooted in the classical historical, biblical, theological, Wesleyan traditions and interpreted for 21st century contexts; able to navigate in a rapidly changing global society

2. Character, vocational and spiritual formation: forming and nurturing the leader as person, in vocational identity and in spiritual practices that nourish holiness of life and heart in leaders and their communities. This would include nourishing healthy relationships and being accountable to peers and superintendents.

3. Skills: forming and nurturing leaders who

   - engage in discernment, both personal and community (attentive to the Holy Spirit and the needs of their communities and congregations)

   - are capable of shaping grace-filled communities that embody the gospel of Jesus Christ and, at the same time, of embracing ministry with and to those outside of the church community

   - are skilled in preaching, leading worship, and communicating through various media

   - embrace styles of leadership that draw others into a life of service

   - are capable of developing intentional processes for making disciples which include engagement with the poor and marginalized

- are able to function in diverse and multicultural settings

- are innovative and missional as they seek to form and nurture communities to new levels of performance and integrity and to reach out to the world beyond the doors of the church

- have the practical wisdom necessary 1) to draw upon a variety of disciplines to lead communities as they navigate conflict and difference in a rapidly changing international and interfaith landscape and 2) to narrate vocation, cast visions, challenge and stimulate Wesleyan understandings of stewardship, and develop human and financial resources to facilitate and sustain faithful, vital, and transforming Christian ministry

Above all of these important skills, principled Christian leaders must be shaped by the grace of God. They will have the love of God poured out into their hearts by the Holy Spirit (Romans 5:5) and will seek to have the same mind in themselves that was in Christ Jesus (Philippians 2:5).

(Used by permission.)

Stage 8: Counseled Again?

SAINT PAUL SCHOOL OF THEOLOGY EXPLAINS ITS RELOCATION TO THE CHURCH OF THE RESURRECTION:

- Create a closer link between academia and church in a groundbreaking collaboration with The United Methodist Church of the Resurrection. No other United Methodist seminary has educationally aligned itself in this way with a church.

- Adapt curriculum and programs to meet the needs of today's church where congregations are comprised of believers who are more intentionally involved instead of merely traditionally present in the mission of the church.

- Make theological degrees more affordable to more students by reallocating our resources and direction more to scholarships and other student support.

- Engage our visionary school in the day-to-day life of a growing, vibrant and vital congregation.

- Provide an active and multilocation congregation—members, leaders, laypeople—access to deeper theological learning opportunities.

- Arm students with practical experience like never before in a variety of worship styles and mission fields.

- Further extend the brand identity of both Saint Paul School of Theology and The United Methodist Church of the Resurrection to expand the reach locally, regionally, nationally and internationally.

- Extend the success of planting our roots in Oklahoma by further extending and diversifying our reach.

- Work with a congregation focused on attracting seekers who are becoming deeply committed Christian disciples in an environment welcoming to nonreligious and nominally religious people.[165]

---

[130] *Proceedings of the Bishop and Presiding Elders of the Methodist-Episcopal Church, in Council Assembled, at Baltimore, on the First Day of December, 1789* (Baltimore: William Woodard and James Angell, 1789). *Minutes; Taken at a Council of the Bishop and Delegated Elders of the Methodist-Episcopal Church: Held at Baltimore in the State of Maryland, December 1, 1790* (Baltimore: W. Goddard and J. Angell, 1790).

[131] Thomas Coke and Francis Asbury. *The Doctrines and Disciplines of the Methodist Episcopal Church, in America* (Philadelphia: Henry Tuckniss, 1798), 77–78, 50, 57, 72, 66–67.

[132] Coke and Asbury, *Doctrines and Discipline* (1798), 83–84.

[133] J. B. Wakeley, *The Patriarch of One Hundred Years: Being Reminiscences, Historical and Biographical, of Rev. Henry Boehm* (New York: Nelson & Phillips, 1875; facsimile reprint ed. Abram W. Sangrey (Lancaster 1982), 60–61.

[134] *A Journal of the Travels of William Colbert, Methodist Preacher: thro' parts of Maryland, Pennsylvania, New York, Delaware and Virginia in 1790 to 1838* (10 volume typescript, used at Drew). 1: 26, 27, 28, 32, 36–37, 39, 40, 41, 55, 73, 74, 77.

[135] A. W. Drury, trans. and ed., *Minutes of the Annual and General Conferences of the Church of the United Brethren in Christ, 1800–1818*. Dayton: Published for the United Brethren Historical Society, 1897. [Consult there to see that the UB began new numbering for successive sessions on a given day and that not all entries are here reproduced. For larger excerpts see MEA 2. There the entire set, 1800-1817, appears as 1800b.]

[136] Coke and Asbury, *Doctrines and Discipline* (1798), 72.

[137] Robert Paine, *Life and Times of William M'Kendree, Bishop of the Methodist Episcopal Church*, 2 vols. (Nashville: Publishing House of the Methodist Episcopal Church, South, 1874), 1: 71.

[138] D. W. Clark, *Life and Times of Rev. Elijah Hedding*. With an Introduction by Rev. Bishop E. S. Janes (New York: Carlton & Phillips, 1855), 134–35.

[139] Hedges, comp. *Crowned Victors*, 185.

[140] Peter Cartwright, *Autobiography of Peter Cartwright: The Backwoods Preacher*, ed. W. P. Strickland (New York: Carlton & Porter, 1857), 78–79.

[141] William F. Warren, "Ministerial Education in Our Church," *Methodist Quarterly Review* 54 (1872): 246–67 (246–51, 253). Warren italicized items 1-3. Quoting his assertions permits reduction in his elaboration and their length.

[142] Nathan Bangs, *A History of the Methodist Episcopal Church*, 8th ed., 4 vols. (New York: Carlton &

Porter, 1860) 3:43–44. Bangs reproduced the whole report of the committee of ways and means.

[143] Baltimore Conference Journal, Ms., 1817, 99–100; quoted by William J. E. Apsley, "The Educational Concerns, 1816–61," in *Those Incredible Methodists. A History of the Baltimore Conference of the United Methodist Church*, Gordon Pratt Baker, ed. (Baltimore: Commission on Archives and History, Baltimore Conference, 1972), 132–33.

[144] *The Methodist Magazine* 12 (1830, new series #1), 392.

[145] La Roy Sunderland, "Essay on a Theological Education," Written by request of the "Junior Preachers' Society" of the New England Conference by Rev. La Roy Sunderland, Member of the said Conference. *The Methodist Magazine* 16 (1834), new series #5, 430.

[146] Ibid. 431.

[147] Ibid. 437.

[148] Bangs, *History*, 3:105B07. The New England Conference dutifully spread the General Conference legislation on its minutes. *See Minutes of the New England Conference of the Methodist Episcopal Church. . . 1766 to . . . 1845*, 1: 301–02 (1820). The Ohio Conference apparently did not get the message. See William Warran Sweet, ed. *Circuit-Rider Days Along the Ohio. Being the Journals of the Ohio Conference from its Organization in 1812 to 1826* (New York and Cincinnati: The Methodist Book Concern, 1923), 185–214.

[149] Edward Otheman, *The Christian Student. Memoir of Isaac Jennison, Jr. Late a Student of the Wesleyan University, Middletown, Conn. Containing his Biography, Diary, and Letters* (New York: G. Lane & P. P. Sandford for the Methodist Episcopal Church, 1843), 38–43. Editor Otheman explained, "The Missionary Lyceum, here mentioned, is an association of students in the Wesleyan University, whose object is to collect missionary intelligence, as also books that will be useful to the religious student, and natural and artificial curiosities from countries visited by missionaries, and to revive and increase among themselves a personal interest in this great and holy cause. For these purposes correspondence is maintained with missionaries and with similar societies, and a suitable room is occupied, where lectures, conversations, and prayers are attended, and a library and museum are kept. It has been the most interesting of all the associations of the students, and has served to foster the spirit of Christian benevolence in many a youthful breast." 40–41.

[150] Edward Otheman, *The Christian Student. Memoir of Isaac Jennison, Jr. Late a Student of the Wesleyan University, Middletown, Conn. Containing his Biography, Diary, and Letters* (New York: G. Lane & P. P. Sandford for the Methodist Episcopal Church, 1843), 38–43.

[151] *Autobiography of Peter Cartwright*, 408. Cartwright continued the retrospective tirade and echoed it elsewhere. See 408–10 and 484–87.

[152] James Strong, "A Central Theological Seminary for Our Church," *Christian Advocate and Journal* 28 (Dec. 22, 1853), 201.

[153] R. S. Foster, *A Treatise on the Need of the M. E. Church with respect to Her Ministry: Embodied in a Sermon, and Preached by Request before the New-York East Conference, May 22, 1855* (New York: Carlton & Phillips, 1855), 13, 54, 58–60.

[154] Review of "*A Treatise on the Need of the Methodist Episcopal Church with Respect to her Ministry*, by R. S. FOSTER, D. D." (New-York: 1855; 18mo., pp. 62.) *Methodist Quarterly Review* 37 (1855), Fourth series 7, 638–40. [638–39].

[155] JGC/MEC 1892: 474.

[156] Franklin C. Woodward, "Methodism and Ministerial Education," *Southern Methodist Review* (Nov. 1886), 208–17; 212, 213, 214, 216, 217.

[157] JGC/MEC 1896: 50.

[158] Robert L. Kelly, *Theological Education in America: A Study of One Hundred Sixty-one Theological Schools in the United States and Canada* (New York: George H. Doran Company, 1924), vii, 97, 98, 99.

[159] William Adams Brown and Mark May, *The Education of American Ministers*, 4 vols. (New York: Institute of Social and Religious Research, 1934), 3: 192-51. On the Brown/May study, see Miller, *Piety and Profession: American Theological Education, 1870-1970*, 470–89.

[160] Brown and May, *The Education of American Ministers*, 3: 35–36.

[161] Ibid. 3: 57–59.

[162] Ibid. 3: 251.

[163] John O. Gross, "The Methodist Church and Theological Education," *The Ministry in the Methodist Heritage*, ed. Gerald O. McCulloh (Nashville: Department of Ministerial Education, 1960), 129-43, 133. The book contained papers presented at a Convocation of Methodist Theological Faculties, including one essay by my father.

[164] See http://www.gbhem.org/sites/default/files/PUB_WESLEYANVISIONTHEOEDUCATION.PDF. Accessed 10/22/2013.

[165] http://www.spst.edu/ Accessed 9/28/13. Used with permission.